# The Complete Perfectionist

EL MÁS FIEL

CANTARON los gallos tristes
como señal del destino,
el hombre se puso en pie,
miró sin sueño al abismo.

—Pero, ante la luz rojiza
que recorté el roto pino,
uno que era diferente,
siguió tendido lo mismo.

Habló el otro que llegó,
vino el animal sumiso,
un humo olía a mujer;
abrió la puerta el camino.

El pájaro, el trigo, el agua,
todo se erguía en lo limpio,
pero no se levantaba
uno, el que era distinto.

(¿Dónde saludaba al pájaro,
dónde oía el arroyillo,
desde dónde se miraba,
como otra espiga, tendido?)

—Pero no se levantaba
uno, el que era distinto,
pero no se levantaba
uno que estaba en su sitio.

Manuscript of the ballad "El más fiel," typewritten with autograph corrections by JRJ. The poem commemorates the death of a nephew in the Spanish Civil War. Juan Ramón Jiménez Bayo, son of Juan Ramón's brother Eustaquio, an officer in Franco's army, died in the battle of Teruel in April 1938.

# The Complete Perfectionist

## A POETICS OF WORK

— ❊ —

JUAN RAMÓN JIMÉNEZ

*Edited & Translated by*

Christopher Maurer

NEW AND REVISED EDITION

Swan Isle Press, Chicago 60640-8790
Edition © 2011 by Swan Isle Press
Spanish original copyright © 2011 by Los herederos de Juan Ramón Jiménez
Essays and Translation © 2011 by Christopher Maurer
All rights reserved. Published 2011
Printed in the United States of America
First Paperback Edition

ISBN-13: 978-0-983-32200-9

English translation of two poems by Juan Ramón Jiménez from *American Poetry: Wildness and Domesticity* by Robert Bly, ©1990 by Robert Bly. Reprinted by permission of HarperCollins Publishers, Inc.

Library of Congress Cataloging-in-Publication Data
Jiménez, Juan Ramón, 1881-1958
The Complete Perfectionist: a poetics of work /
Juan Ramón Jiménez ;
edited and translated by Christopher Maurer. —
1st paperback ed.; New and rev. ed.    p. cm.
Includes bibliographical references.
ISBN-13: 978-098-332200-9  (alk. paper)
1. Work. 2. Perfection 3. Jiménez, Juan Ramón, 1881-1958
1. Maurer, Christopher. II. Title.
BJ1498.J55 2012    861'.62--dc23    2011037107

Swan Isle Press gratefully acknowledges that this book has been made possible, in part, with the support of generous grants from:

PROGRAM FOR CULTURAL COOPERATION BETWEEN SPAIN'S
MINISTRY OF CULTURE AND UNITED STATES UNIVERSITIES

EUROPE BAY GIVING TRUST

FRONTISPIECE: Manuscript of the ballad "El más fiel," typewritten with autograph corrections by JRJ. Published in *Romances de Coral Gables (1939–42)*. Facsimile courtesy of Sala Zenobia/Juan Ramón Jiménez, Universidad de Puerto Rico, Río Piedras.

*www.swanislepress.com*

*for María Estrella*

# Contents

*Introduction*  1

Self  17

Rhythm  27

Silence  39

The Present  51

Memory  59

Ideals  65

Nature  73

Instinct  85

Dream  93

Death  103

Writing  113

Revision  125

Perfection  139

*Afterword*  147

*Sources & Acknowledgements*  153

# Introduction

FROM THE PRINTER a long-awaited package: the first copies of one of his books. Fine paper, clear type, generous margins. Near the title page is a gracefully drawn sprig of parsley—his emblem of simplicity. He has written and designed the entire book in a dream of poetical and typographical perfection: "naked poetry," elegant on the page.

Before others have read it, perhaps even before they have cut its pages, one of those copies is in ruins. Torn from its binding, it lies on a table crowded with his papers. Here and there, a title has been replaced with a better one, a line of verse has been canceled, the margins bristle with notes.

"When I publish a book I'm never happy," he writes. "On the contrary, the moment I receive the first printed copy ...I tear off the cover and begin all over again. Letting go of a book is always, for me, a provisional solution, reached on a day of weakness."

He is, unmistakably, a perfectionist—the "complete perfectionist" of our title. Juan Ramón Jiménez (1881-1958), maker of poems and aphorisms, master of several generations

3

of Spanish poets, winner of a Nobel Prize for Literature.

Few writers have yearned more intensely for perfection, defined it more carefully, or spoken so lucidly of their struggle to achieve it, one day after another, over an entire creative lifetime. In these pages, drawn from several of his books, Juan Ramón reaches beyond ordinary notions of "quality" or "excellence"; reaches from the work of poetry to what he calls "the poetry of work": work so right, so instinct with surprise and beauty that it strikes us as "fatal" and perfect.

In *The Complete Perfectionist* I have tried to gather into a "poetics of work"—a system of guiding principles—the thought of a master poet and master worker. One by one, Juan Ramón takes up the essential elements of work: time and rhythm, noise and silence, the power to remember and the ability to forget. He teaches us to live contentedly within the present; listen more attentively to instinct; draw strength from dream and reverie; measure our work against the quiet steady work of nature; and calm the fear of death with trust in our daily labor.

Juan Ramón offers a vision of perfection not as an abstract, distant goal, and not as the absence of defects, but as an "unending fervor" that enlivens the hourly and daily course of work. For him, perfection is always a matter of becoming. It lies not in the past but in the present; never in what he has done, and always in what he is doing. It is more of a path than a goal, the process of making rather than the thing made. Perfection is "ecstasy" and restless movement. It can only be caught "in motion" and "in progress."

Juan Ramón's vision of perfection arose from sixty years of experience as a careful maker of poems. "Let us think more with our hands!" he once wrote. But it is also a proudly idealistic vision.

"Mankind," he writes, "has become excessively realistic": "life (and death) are not what we read about in the news-papers." In poetry and in work, he pursues the essences of things, and few writers have ever lived more confidently and contentedly in the realm of desire and imagination.

> It seems more logical to live so-called reality than so-called reverie. But at death more truth and life remain of those who lived their reverie, than of those who chased after that reality.

In the arduous daily work of his poetry— his "discipline and oasis," his "caprice and crucible"—he cannot help looking beyond the freshly printed book, the pages awaiting revision on his table. "I want to look at things, but I only see through them." In all that he looks at lies something infinitely better.

## SOLITUDE AND PUBLIC LIFE

HIS DREAM OF perfect work was nurtured in solitude, but through it he hoped to leave a lasting effect on the Spanish language, on poetry, and on society: good work, like good poetry, is "contagious." It begins in a quiet room, has an ef-fect on others, and transforms public life. Deep social change can arise from a single person's thirst for perfection.

His quest can be explained, in part, by historical circum-stance. When he left his native Andalusia in 1900 and made his first trip to Madrid, Spain was recovering from catastro-phe. Two years earlier, she had been soundly defeated by the U.S. and had lost Cuba, Puerto Rico, and the Philippines, and that humiliation had touched off an intense public debate about her future. Two issues in particular affected the course of Juan Ramón's creative life: the need to recreate Spanish poetry and to rebuild Spain through work.

He sensed, to begin with, that one could not "remake" one's country without remaking her language and that the best way to change language is through poetry. A great poet—the one Juan Ramón hoped to become—alters common language and, with it, social thought and feeling. Change the way people speak and you will change the way they act. After the disaster of 1898, it seemed urgent to set aside the bombast of imperial Spain—a Spain that had ceased to exist—and to speak more quietly and intimately. Poetry, the highest, most memorable form of speech, had spent too much time in pulpits, barracks, and public places. Juan Ramón wanted to build her a "house of time and silence."

> I dreamed for our language a poetry that would be both ideal and material, spiritual and sensual, melodious, lovely, mysterious, enchantingly universal, like the best of ancient Greek, Indian, Chinese or Arabic poetry, or modern English, with less rhetoric and less nationalism; poetry of an altogether higher order, with more breeze and more freedom. A constant poetry, like the one sought by St. John of the Cross and [Gustavo Adolfo] Bécquer, but more abundant and richer.

In his hands, Spanish prose became more supple and suggestive. Poetry in Spanish lay aside certain habits of declamation, sharpened its five senses, and entered transcendental realms little explored until then. No one since Góngora had lavished such care on his language, and no poet since St. John of the

Cross had written about ecstasy so simply and precisely.

The lifelong effort to recreate Spanish language and poetry arose from Juan Ramón's faith in the power of work to renew both the individual and society. Overwhelmingly, the writers of his generation, from Miguel de Unamuno and José Ortega y Gasset to Antonio Machado and Pío Baroja, portray Spaniards as stricken with *abulia*: spiritual and physical listlessness. It seemed that, at a moment no one could remember—a moment uncannily similar to our own—Spain had lost her will to work. Above all, Juan Ramón thought, she had better learn respect for intellectual labor and the pursuit of beauty.

> O pure Beauty—poetry, art, science—how are you to live in
> my country, without respect and without silence; live with
> some of these inferior animals who peer through the keyhole
> to see you going by, like Lady Godiva, tender, sad naked!

"If God were, and were a Spaniard," he joked, "it would take less than a month for people to lose all respect for Him." The work he took upon himself, as a young man, was "to impose, with all my spirit, all that is refined, delicate and exquisite about Spain over whatever is coarse, ugly and unpleasant."

Defending his solitude, keeping at bay the raw "materialism" of Spain and the world, Juan Ramón tried to make his life a radiant example of *el trabajo gustoso*: work embraced willingly, with pleasure and delight. Spain was not going to be made on a street corner or in a café or in the newspapers, he said, and reflected that if his country was to rise again proudly from a "foundation of good granite and myrtle," there must be a few hundred people working passionately to set the tone for others.

In his youth, reading Shelley, Juan Ramón underlined the famous dictum, "Poets are the unacknowledged legislators of the world." He would spend his life attempting to practice a "political poetics" or "ethical aesthetics": an art without an explicitly political message but one with deep and subtle effects upon public sensibility. Every day he felt more certain that social improvement would come not from programs of public reform, not from "those unforgivably amateur actors," the "political phantoms who rule us." It would come instead, from a small but growing elite of individual workers, an "immense minority," each of whom loved his own livelihood and delighted in his own daily work:

> Constant, endless fervor
> of my work.
> Restlessness
> held in a chalice...!

> Burning wave, feeling
> and fire, in the goblet
> of a happy will.

Part of his own work lay in teaching, and to younger poets he was a devoted and generous mentor. He prepared the way for them, reviving all the forms of Spanish poetry, from the folk song and *romance* to the sonnet or prose poem. Alluding to that formal renewal, Robert Bly says that Juan Ramón opened up new paths of association and "threw up light and airy houses made out of willows, and in so many different designs that all the coming Spanish poets found themselves living in one or another of his willow houses before they moved out to their own." An excellent group of poets came to maturity under his tutelage: Jorge Guillén, Pedro Salinas, Luis Cernuda, Federico García Lorca, Rafael Alberti, Gerardo Diego, Vicente Aleixandre. Lorca called him a "master," and it was partly thanks to Juan Ramón that he could declare proudly in 1935, a year before the outbreak of the Civil War, that Spanish poetry was the finest being written in Europe. Juan Ramón taught his disciples never to hurry; not to court the multitude (he never forgave Lorca for writing plays); and to accept responsibility for all aspects of their work, from its conception to its careful revision and its appearance on the printed page. He taught them to read one another with attention. Above all, he taught them to live their lives for poetry alone, to live poetry as an all-embracing passion in which they could "burn completely."

He was, perhaps, too stern a teacher, too implacable a defender of his own vision of poetry, one which valued emotion and "accent" more than the lightning bolt of metaphor, and it was not long before he was at odds with almost all of his disciples. In a series of pen portraits, he sharpened his prose on their weaknesses until he found himself nearly totally alone, and quoting the Spanish proverb, "Bring up ravens and they will eat out your eyes." "They will eat out my eyes," he wrote bitterly, "because my eyes [still] give them nourishment." It was an ugly struggle, but not a useless one: he did, after all, impart to his disciples his own fierce sense of independence. "The job of a poet," he said, "is not to kill poets by creating disciples," but the other way around, "to create poets by killing disciples or himself. Whether killing himself or his disciples, what the true poet gives is life, not death like the supposed 'master.'"


## STRUGGLING WITH THE PAGE

LIKE ANY PERFECTIONIST, Juan Ramón was unimaginably difficult to live with, and the tangle of his eccentricities—his *cosas*—sometimes exasperated even his wife, Zenobia Camprubí, whose cheer, strength and devotion were legendary. How often she must have smiled ironically, collected her things, and gone off to see friends or out on business, closing—sometimes slamming—the door on his imagined ailments, his hatred of noise, his allergies, his need for "outer order and spiritual restlessness."

One of his peculiarities—to him it was a curse—was that he could not stop writing: poems in verse and in prose, aphorisms, lectures, critical essays, letters, translations of Yeats and Blake, Shakespeare and Shelley, and (with Zenobia) many volumes of the Hindu poet Tagore, including the latter's aphorisms, *Stray Birds*. His abundance, unrivalled by any major Spanish poet, kept him in anguish over the revision, arrangement, and publication of his work. The central drama of his life was this struggle with the page: "the printed page and the empty one!"

He had avid readers... but how to place his poems in their hands, how to reach his own "immense minority"? He was content at first to publish books of poems: fifteen of them by 1916, another seven by 1923.[1] Those individual books were revised and transformed, sensibly enough, into volumes

[1] Two of the best known, and perhaps best, were *Platero y yo (Platero and I)*, a book of elegiac prose poems about a young man's love for his donkey and for their Andalusian surroundings, and *Diario de un poeta reciencasado (Diary of a Newly Married Poet)*, inspired by a sea voyage to the U.S. where he met Zenobia.

of selected verse (his personal *antologías*). But such partial offerings were never able to keep pace with the rhythm of his work (for years, from one to three poems per day), and over the years he turned despairingly from one solution to another. He brought out several series of exquisite *cuadernos*: pamphlets or *plaquettes* combining his own work with that of younger poets and artists. Perfect, but too expensive! He resigned himself to seeing his poems and prose in the daily newspapers: worn, ugly typefaces, humiliating misprints (*cosa* or *rosa*?), the nasty proximity of ads for cough medicine and lice repellent. He thought of finding an obedient printer and paying him to print up his daily work (fifty copies would do), or of buying a printing press and installing it in his basement. These were provisional measures. They arose from his belief that a poet should work and produce continuously, following his own "vegetative rhythm," like a "gentle force of nature." From about 1924, he felt certain that what mattered was his work as a whole: not his "collected poems," not his *obras*, his works, but his *Obra*, with a capital letter, in the singular: the book to end all books and restore the universe to silence. That Work would be all presence. He wanted to revise his work entirely into the present, reliving it as he revised, in order to feel again, in a single, eternal moment, every poem he had ever written. Like a god, he would be fully conscious, at once, of his entire creation.

> I would like my book
> to be like the sky at night,
> all present truth, without history.
>
> I want it, like the sky,

to give itself fully at each instant
with all its stars [...]

His ideas on how to bring that "total" book into material existence changed incessantly over the years. It would form one organic work of poetry and prose, *Metamorphosis*, in twenty-one? fourteen? in seven volumes, beginning with a galaxy of aphorisms (*Ideolojía*) and ending with the sources of his poems and the efforts of his imitators (among his papers are parts of an anthology with acute and nasty comments, entitled *My Best Echo*). It was a project too vast for any one life, and he was often overwhelmed by depression. His daily struggle for wholeness, his longing for completion, brought him face to face with his own mortality, and it isn't surprising that he devoted so much thought to death, teaching himself to accept it calmly as an element in the total equation of his work.

In 1936, on the outbreak of the Civil War, Juan Ramón was named Cultural Attaché of the Spanish Embassy in Washington, and, in voluntary exile, was separated from his books and papers. In his Madrid apartment, exposed to destruction and theft, he had left the entire "rough draft" of his *Obra*: thousands of pages of poetry, personal correspondence, and notes. And yet in exile his work flowered once again in poetry and prose—seven more published books—about the god within him and the immanence of that god in nature. Some of his masterpieces from that period were *Dios deseado y deseante* (God Desired and Desiring), *Espacio* (Space), *Tiempo* (Time), and *Españoles de tres mundos* (Spaniards of Three Worlds), a collection of piquant pen portraits, the best biographical prose ever written by a Spaniard.

An enemy of fascism, he refused to return to Franco's Spain, and spent the last twenty years of his life in New York, Havana, Riverdale (Maryland), Coral Gables, and finally, San Juan, Puerto Rico, where he and Zenobia received word in 1956 that he had been awarded the Nobel Prize for Literature for having given the world "an inspiring example of spirituality and artistic purity." The honor meant almost nothing to him. Zenobia was suffering atrociously, and died from cancer three days after the announcement. He was defeated by her death: for forty years, she had been his constant companion, transcribing his work, solving the problems of daily life and allowing him to concentrate fully on his poetry. Unable to write more, he died himself a year and a half later.

## THE QUEST FOR BREVITY

AS EARLY AS 1900 he had begun to write aphorisms, and by the time of his death, had accumulated more than four thousand of them. The aphorism seemed to summon perfection and challenge it; it is both easier and harder to be perfect in a few words than in many. It was also, like the short poem, a sign of reverence for silence. Speak exactly and you will speak less, perhaps not at all. So much the better: "better to be silent than speak." In his writing, Juan Ramón, like Mallarmé, wished to create a perfect universe where writing and speech are unnecessary: "Writing poetry is preparation for unwritten poetry." To him, the aphorism represented a "concession," it was what you did "in the meantime."

So as not to argue with myself about the conviction, the

duty, the need not to write anymore, I write all the time, at every moment. As a friendly concession to the writer in me, I write the aphorism, the short poem, the song, the epigram.

Often, he tells us, he grew tired of discursive prose and tired of reading novels and plays that take us on a "more or less lyrical detour," only to lead back to "the life from which we were trying to escape." He loved brevity and the "surprise of sudden illumination." There were times when he thought the world would be a more civilized, considerate place if poet, philosopher and historian went straight to the point. Not that there wasn't room for "stentorian poets of laughter and wailing, but

> Who says there can't be a place also, for quiet, serene ones, for when we need quiet and serenity? Ah, to be one of them! One of the poets whose song helps close the wound rather than open it!

### POETRY AND WORK

This book, the first collection in English of Juan Ramón's aphorisms, offers a lifetime of wise, often whimsical observations about "perfect" writing and perfect work. The word poet means "maker," and the assumption, in these pages, is that a master poet can offer insight into the nature of work, freeing it from its "institutional" or business framework, and allowing his readers to meditate about work the way one meditates about love apart from the social institution of marriage. Seen from the vantage point of poetry, work touches on everything that matters. It gives life rhythm, deepens appreciation of silence, nature and dream, brings the present into vivid existence, and consoles us for being mortal.

This is a book of suggestions, rather than of instruction or advice. Like any teacher, Juan Ramón liked to give advice, but in his aphorisms he sometimes draws back from doing so: "Let no one take advice from this book; the only thing that matters is one's own experience." Again: "These aphorisms are neither law or rule for anyone, not even for me. They are merely enjoyable, sensual, whimsical deductions." Juan Ramón was an individualist, intent on his own perfection, and these pages often show him in dialogue with himself rather than with the reader. There *is* much advice about work in this book, but it is not always delivered in the second person. The *you* is sometimes *him*, not us. Juan Ramón wondered whether art can instruct at all:

> Art is not actively didactic, no. But it is clear that the perfect fruit of the cultivated spirit—a spirit intent only upon its own perfection—can educate others through that very perfection.

How, then, apply these aphorisms to writing and to work? Each chapter of this book deals with an element of work. But within each chapter, the aphorisms, and occasionally short poems, go off in their own directions, without following a rigid line of reasoning, sometimes with a touch of mystery, without declaring their meaning. "Between idea and idea, a dream!" Juan Ramón did not like the idea of laboring over a poem—or, presumably, an aphorism—to get at its meaning ("Sad flower, forced open!"):

> When I don't understand a poem or part of it, I don't insist; I try to be satisfied with what I understand, and I'm sure

that another time, under other conditions, I'll understand more and understand something else ...the understanding of a poem comes in successive surprises.

As editor and translator, I hope that these aphorisms, too, will lead to "successive surprises." Reading them requires an imaginative leap from poetry to other forms of work. To make that leap, the reader must make a running start on one side or the other, and either truly love poetry or love his work. Auguste Rodin, who was in love with sculpture, describes such a leap in his own reading:

Whoever understands one thing, understands all, for the same laws are in everything. I have learned sculpture and have known well that that was something great. I recall that once when I was reading *The Imitation of Christ*, especially in the third book, I replaced the word "God" everywhere with "sculpture," and it worked, and it was right.

Here, then, are the words of a great worker: sparks from his anvil, his poetics of work.

# Self

*Quiero ser, a un tiempo, la flecha y el
punto donde se clava... o se pierde.*

—JRJ

ONE OF JUAN RAMÓN'S best known works in progress was his *I*, his public self. Over the years, in a series of vignettes and aphorisms, he portrayed himself as god, as nature, as his own disciple and master; in short, as a sufficient, alternate universe.

Like his poetry, that *I*, that public ego, was in a constant state of revision. In his earliest poses for the photographer, one sees the sad, dark eyes of a self-declared "martyr of Beauty," a "precision instrument for thinking and feeling." The well-trimmed beard and elegant attire suggest a master of perfection: "My kingdom lies in the difficult." His look could be sharp, fastidious, challenging, and one or two of the photos might have been inscribed with the aphorism "Let us cultivate, before all else, the will to reject!" On an imaginary calling card—one of many he handed to posterity—he engraved the words

THE UNIVERSAL ANDALUSIAN

In one of his autobiographical pen portraits, he catches his reflection in a windowpane and finds that his head "bears a stunning resemblance to those of Góngora, Calderón, and Shakespeare."

Not surprisingly, his enemies called him Narcissus. They were right, he replied. All gods, and therefore all poets, fall in love with their own creation; and all male creators fall in love with the poetic, feminine side of themselves. But Narcissus, too, was misunderstood. What he saw in the water was an image not of himself but of completion and worldly beauty. When he peered into the pool, into the very "eye of Nature," Narcissus longed to escape from himself and dissolve into the universe: the noblest sort of metamorphosis. More stinging than "Narcissus," Juan Ramón thought, were the names his mother called him as a child: "Juanito the Demanding. Johnny the Question Mark. Little Mr. Spoiled. The Interrupter, John-John the Whimster, Mr. Invention, Madman, the Exaggerator, Whiner, Pest... Prince."

Was it really *him*, that *I*, spiraling around itself like a Baroque column? Why did he show it so insistently in public, in newspapers and poetry magazines, where it was sure to awaken hostility to his poems and lend itself to ridicule "by different categories of reptiles"? He called himself both a Classic and a Romantic. The Romantic project of his life—his Work, his *Obra*—required a hero, and especially when he was young, the hero needed to be misunderstood by a rude and hostile world. Where no hostility existed, it had to be provoked or teased into existence. It was fun baiting others with those public "selves," chuckling at the idiots who took them too seriously. So many Juan Ramóns in search of perfection! There is the *I* of some of the autobiographical aphorisms: the proud martyr of Beauty, the Universal Andalusian. There is the ecstatic *I* of the poems, the selfless Narcissus in love with solitude and the beauty of the world. And there is the worker, the humble *me* who wrote the other two into existence: the *exijente*[1] who struggled endlessly to write perfectly. Life in exile brought another sort of fragmentation. In the United States and Puerto Rico, Juan Ramón heard himself speak in the tongue of another, and heard others speak in a tongue that was, and wasn't, his own." I no longer trust myself, and no longer trust what I now read written in Spanish in Spain and outside of Spain, and if I want to remember, think, criticize the Spanish of Spaniards I no longer know what I read or what I speak or what I write."

Those selves are not easily reconciled, and it is not always easy to distinguish public and private. Identity is the deepest of human mysteries, and no identity is more mysterious than that of someone whose life is his art. "To live is to create, and re-create, ourselves," he wrote. No final solution is possible, no identity definitive. It would be harder to imagine an artist of greater integrity. But the notion of identity—of remaining "the very same" person—was alien to him. Here, as elsewhere in his thought, perfection lies in succession, transition, metamorphosis:

> To poetize is to become a new I each day in a new vision and expression of myself and of the world that I see, my world …This passing of the torch from one I to another, and from me to the person who follows, these stages in a beautiful

---

[1] The normal spelling is exigente, but one of Juan Ramón's eccentricities was to write *j*, and not *g*, before an *i* or an *e*.

career of light, are the way I conceive of life.

Juan Ramón loved the idea of life as orbit: "We are nothing but orbit walkers. We can never reach an end, never reach ourselves, unless our end is, simply, to run after ourselves."

One of the names he gave himself was *El Cansado de su Nombre* (Tired of His Name). We can imagine that, in life and in art, he grew tired of himself and his names: tired, even, of his pronouns.

> I am not I.
>                     I am this one
> Walking beside me whom I do not see.
> Whom at times I manage to visit.
> And at other times I forget.
> The one who remains silent when I talk.
> The one who forgives, sweet, when I hate.
> The one who takes a walk when I am indoors.
> The one who will remain standing when I die.
>
> (TRANSLATED BY ROBERT BLY)

— ❋ —

Nature has given me two irreconcilable virtues: supreme productivity and the yearning for supreme perfection ... Thus my martyrdom—for Beauty—and my melancholy.

What a struggle within me between the complete and the perfect!

What a great thing it is: to be absolute master of perfection and scorn it like this!

### Narcissist?

Every true poet is a Narcissist, for the true poet is a contemplative and a creator. God is Narcissus. The men who have taken themselves to be Gods— Christ, Buddha—are Narcissists. This makes sense because what a poet tries to do is create a world of his own and thus looks at himself in the world; not in water, but in all of nature, earth, fire, air, and everything else.

Narcissus is the whole and he is eternity. If a poet leaves himself and merely echoes life, he ceases immediately to be a poet. For life is a derived event and the poet is the creator of life.

Narcissus loves life, but loves it in himself because he has all of life inside him.

### Relation

I have poetry hidden in my house, for her pleasure and mine. And our relation is one of passion.

I would give the better half of my work not to have written the other.

My best work is my constant repentance for my Work.

I am eternal. I have no possible solution.

I am so abstracted in the eternal that spiders have woven

their cobwebs between my feet.

I want to be at the same time the arrow and the target it goes through... or where it gets lost.

I like not the event but its representation. For in the event I am only a participant or a spectator and in the representation of it I am a creator; that is, a poet.

### Not doing them

They ask me, "Why don't you do this thing or that?"
I answer, "Because what keeps me alive is precisely not doing them. I live negating their affirmation or affirming their negation."

They say I am monotonous. Right. All I sing is the universe!

My only two weapons: time and silence.

My life is constant regret for not having done things I refused to do when I could have.

To disorder my inner life, I have to tidy up my outer one.

I don't smoke, don't drink wine, hate coffee and bullfighting, religion and militarism, the accordion and the death penalty. I live only for, and by, Beauty...

I love outer order and spiritual restlessness.

They call my work unreal. Unreal, yes. But quiet and eternal in the madness of life, like the shadow of a castle in the stream that tries to carry it away.

Some of my affectionate envious friends say, "You write too much."

"Maybe," I answer. "But as long as the best of your little is worse than the worst of my much, I'll keep on doing so."

I believe in the "great poet," who isn't the one who reaches the widest public but the one who creates the most public.

Even greater would be the poet who could build the total, immense minority.

That is my own illusion.

"Glory" (what a word!) consists in going from the me that others don't know to the other me that I don't know.

### True and same

To flee always from oneself, from others, and from the other, in order to be always... true and same.

### You are old

If a child calls you old, you are old; if a woman calls you young, you are old; if you aren't sure whether you're old or young, you are old.

The Universal Andalusian.

Tired of his Name.

Lovable and inflexible.

### *In the end*

Hidden creator of an unapplauded star.

# Rhythm

*¡Días 'perdidos' tan llenos de hallazgos!*
— J R J

TWO OF THE basic elements of work are time and rhythm. Without the freedom to master these and use them wisely, there can be no happiness in work and no perfection, only the monotony of alienated labor. There is another related element to which Juan Ramón devoted much thought: tempo, the deliberate quickness or slowness of what we are doing. His advice, always, is to "go slowly in art ... don't try to race ahead of the hours." Again and again he returns to the paradoxical formula, "Slowly, you will do everything quickly."

For Juan Ramón, perfect work depends upon a vivid sense of wholeness. A year, season, month, day and hour of work are complete in themselves but felt as part of something larger. "I don't divide up my life into days but my days into lives; each day, each hour [is] an entire life," to be used as fully as possible. His need to imagine his life's work as an entirety made him compare each period of it to a movement in a symphony. It is an ambitious analogy, but a good one, for work, like poetry and music, endows time with rhythm. In fact, rhythm is the meaning given to time, and the right

rhythm of work gives meaning and wholeness to our work-
days and our lives.

But that, of course, requires freedom and fortune. For
those working against time, the hour is a rented room
and the landlord is implacable. In 1934-35, as Juan Ramón
worked incessantly on his poetry and his poetics, the French
philosopher Simone Weil, on a year's leave from the lycée
where she was teaching, had taken a job at a factory in order to experience firsthand the plight of France's industrial
workers. What she noticed about time and rhythm con-
forms exactly to the thought of Juan Ramón. "Time and
rhythm constitute the most important factor of the whole
problem of work," she wrote. "[Our] thought was intended
to master time, and this vocation ...must be kept inviolate
in every man." Weil was observing assembly-line workers
called upon "to execute at high speed, in a specified order,
five or six simple movements, indefinitely repeated, each
lasting a second or thereabouts." The lessons she drew from
the experience are as applicable to intellectual labor as they
are to physical.

> The succession of their movements is not designated in fac-
> tory parlance by the word "rhythm," but by "cadence." This
> is only right, for that succession is the contrary of rhythm.
> Any series of movements that participates of the beautiful
> and is accomplished with no loss of dignity implies moments
> of pause, as short-lived as lightning flashes, but that are the
> very stuff of rhythm and give the beholder, even across ex-
> tremes of rapidity, the impression of leisureliness. The foot
> racer, at the moment of beating the world's record, seems
> to glide home slowly while one watches his inferior rivals

making haste behind him. The better and more swiftly a peasant swings his scythe the more the onlookers have the impression that, as the invariable phrase goes, he is taking his time. On the other hand, the spectacle presented by men over machines is nearly always one of wretched haste destitute of all grace and dignity. It comes naturally to a man, and it befits him, to pause on having finished something, if only for an instant, in order to contemplate his handiwork, as God did in Genesis. Those lightning moments of thought, of immobility and equilibrium, one has to learn to eliminate utterly in a working day at the factory.

The momentary "pause on having finished something," the pause that distinguishes workers from animate tools, is the moment Juan Ramón refers to as "revision," and the ideal rhythm Weil writes about resembles the one he pursued in his own daily work. Like all perfectionists, Juan Ramón worried that his own internal rhythm—his "ideal day" as a worker—did not often correspond to the hours of the clock: "I cannot divide the day into twenty-four hours or twelve. Some of my days have half an hour, and others three, and others a thousand." He is absorbed in the present of his work, and clock time passes him by unnoticed or breaks into his thought like an unwanted noise or guest. He longs for total concentration in all that he does (see "Silence" and "The Present"), and to reach that inner stillness, there can be no urgency to "finish," no regret for yesterday's failures, no "nostalgia for past, pleasurable hours," only new hours of pleasure in the present. Intent upon his work, he begins each morning with his own version of "one day at a time": "Morning prayer: 'Keep things from sticking to me, dawn! Let this day be only today!'" A day, he thought, should be only a day, like an island in the sea of time. He dreamt of making each hour "a round, smooth, well-defined thing which does not go poking into the hour beside it." And yet, when the days or hours are placed beside one another, they ought to bear fruit or procreate, "like male and female in heat."

He struggled endlessly against his own desire to be done in a hurry and against his longing to be working on something else, and he inscribed on the title page of some of his books a thought from Goethe: "Like a star, without haste, but without rest, let man revolve around his work." He tried to find a common rhythm for his days of creation and his days of revision or idleness. Here, as in all he did, he tried to draw inspiration from the slow, successive rhythms of the tides and the seasons. He dreamed that, thanks to his faithful daily rhythm, he would leave the world having spent all of himself on his work, having "emptied" himself into it. He smiled to think that, when worn out by work, there would be nothing left of him for death to claim: "Day after day, I have been putting my whole life into my work. Death? 'I' will not be buried. Only my shell will go down to the earth." What of the "pause" mentioned by Simone Weil? Here is the way he imagined such a moment, on the last day of his life, in the confidence that his work had been completed.

> That day, that day
> when I look at the sea—the two of us calm—
> trusting in it; all my soul
> emptied fully into my Work—
> forever certain, like a great tree
> on the coast of the world,

with its certain leaves and certain roots,
and the great work that is finished!

    That day, when
to sail will be to rest, when I have worked
on me so much, so much, so much!

    That day, that day
when death—black waves—no longer courts me
and I smile endlessly on everything
knowing I leave so little
—just the bare bones—
so very little of myself.


— ※ —


Work, solitude, time.

All the work of the universe is no more than time and
rhythm, rhythm and time. Balance and a means to make
that balance.

The poet's rhythm can be none other than the puls-
ing of his blood at any given moment. Any other external
rhythm—music, the ticking of a clock, a song— throws off
the idea and feeling; that is why he needs silence.


### No better rhythm

For life no rhythm is better than that of thought, for that
rhythm can last through our entire orbit.

## *Rhythm*

Of all the rhythms in the world, the most harmonious is—can be—that of our own lives.

Whoever finds it is happy in body and soul and gives that bodily and spiritual happiness to others.

My "aloofness," my "resonant solitude," the "golden silence" others have always reproached me for and forced on me in a supposed "ivory tower" that I always kept in a corner of my house and never used... I didn't learn those things from some false sense of aristocracy but from the only true aristocracy.

I learned them when I was a child, in Moguer, from the field hand, the carpenter, the knife sharpener, the saddle maker, the mason, and the sailor who worked, alone, on their land, their workshop, or their ship, with body and soul and above all on Sundays, out of truth and faith and joy in their slow, daily pleasurable work.

Let man revolve around his work like a star, without haste but without rest. (Goethe)

A slow haste.

No better way to get there late than to be in a hurry.

Go slowly in art: let each hour give itself to you. Don't try to race ahead of the hours.

What a pleasure to isolate the day! Like a life in the sea

of time, between its morning and its night!

The hour! If someone could teach me to isolate the hour!

How to give the same dimension, always, to every hour into which we distribute the day?

How can we make an hour an hour; a smooth, round, well-defined thing that does not go poking into the hour beside it?

In my day the neighboring hours are like male and female in heat.

> *For Miss Rápida*
> If you go quickly,
> time will fly before you,
> like a butterfly.
>
> If you go slowly,
> time will follow
> like a gentle ox.

No hurry at all. If, in my day, I give each thing—creation, reading, meditation, nature, etc.—all the hours I can and should, that is enough.

No matter how convinced we are that the world is fleeting, let us give each thing, however small, the passion of permanence.

### You will

Slowly, you will do everything quickly.

Spring comes back sooner each year. How will I catch up with the rose?

### Very well made

To work isn't to do a lot in a hurry or, above all, many times; it is to make unique, very well made things.

Doing things badly does not give you the right to demand haste from the person who does them well.

Let's not force things, but let everything arrive at its own moment, in its own peculiar manner, fusing its rhythms with ours.

My books have never run after fame: each of them has arisen from its own place at its own hour.

### Which rhythm?

What a struggle between my two rhythms, the whimsical and the normal. Which should conquer me, which be conquered?

Work, like life, is resolved successively.

From one thing to another, for a change of rhythm. And

careful with those runaway rhythms that send us wheeling downhill!

Every day I draw up a plan, and by the next day I have abandoned it. My soul is covered with useless tattoos.

"Lost" days, so full of finds!

In the work of the intellect, one should have, from time to time, a day of synthesis, analyzing and polishing the labor of days past: something like the beginning of a new life.

We ought to learn the marvelous rhythm of "meanwhile..."

Sometimes I think I'm caressing an idea, and I am caressing a rhythm.

When an extraneous rhythm—or arrhythmia—steals away the rhythm of my work, I have to recover it, tapping my foot on my head!

To work, to work even at night, so my eyes will be worn out when they go back to the earth!

---✻---

# Silence

*¡Qué de silencios desaprovechados en la vida!*
—JRJ

---✻---

GOOD WORK COMES from silence; not necessarily from noiselessness but from the fervent concentration of which silence is an image. Silence is oneness and wholeness. For Juan Ramón, noise leads to dispersion: it "shatters my day and my brain into a thousand little pieces…"

> With silence, I bind up the day, I fuse it into a unity. With noise I go bouncing through the day like a train, from one car to another, stunned and irritated.

Silence is deafness to distraction, to noise in the head; the sting of yesterday's insult, plans for the future. It is deafness to all that makes it impossible to hear and follow the rhythm of our work, and in fact, in a subtle way, some work, like some music or poetry—Juan Ramón's, for example—sharpens one's awareness of silence. The poem, the sonata, the well-made object deepens silence, making it almost palpable. Silence pulses with form. What we see on the lips of the Mona Lisa, Juan Ramón said, is "the melody of silence."

Not only his own poetry but his comments about the work of others show that he was unusually sensitive to the sound of poems. When he speaks about the noises he loves, he speaks of "the verses of a poet, which hardly make any sound along the edge, with all the sound at the center." He is alluding to his love of assonance: the gentle sound of vowels rather than the chime of both vowels and consonants. He is remembering how Cordelia, in *King Lear*, scorns the hollow eloquence of her sisters and wishes only to "love, and be silent." As a poet, he thought often about her apology for silence and simplicity:

Nor are those empty-hearted whose low sounds
Reverb no hollowness.

In his later years, in exile, he transcribed hundreds of pages of his verse into prose, "with all the sound at the center" rather than at the end of the line. "The word," he wrote, "was made for the ear, and not the eye." And he told a friend, pressing the point after a recital he had given for some blind children in Puerto Rico, "take a poem and recite it, and pretend that your listeners are blind."

To hear the sound of his poems and those of others and the counterpoint of his own thought, he needed more silence than Madrid or his own fortitude could provide. The noises around him, the loudspeakers of movie houses, the cries of street vendors, the seventy-year-old woman—the landlady herself!—learning to sing in the apartment under his, made him think bitterly about his country's scorn for intellectual labor. "My effort to reach ethical and aesthetic perfection is enormous; but the effort of everyone else to prevent me from succeeding is infinitely greater." He was engaged, he thought, in giving Spain her first "universal poet." Why couldn't Spain keep quiet?

Parrots on balconies, phonographs, bad pianos (and good ones, badly played), absurd songs, people shouting, doors slamming, street hawkers, crickets in cages, heavy footsteps, dancing in apartments, cold everywhere in winter, unavoidable heat in summer, no opening the windows in spring, in fall, the dry leaves my eyes can't stand, bursts of laughter, eternally crying children and the anonymous hands that spank them, friends with nothing to do, mud, dust, envy, sordidness, hollow beauty, useless wealth, poverty in a corner, the laying out of the body and the orphaned soul. Spain! And the contemplative, universal man who loves you, who has no money, and who ought not or cannot flee from you!

There was nothing he could do about the noisy flock of sparrows under his window (in one apartment he looked down onto the trees in the courtyard of a sanatorium where he had lived years earlier) but what of the people around him? He spoke with envy of a certain legendary cork-lined room (France seemed kinder to her writers) and he consulted with carpenters. His faithful chronicler, Juan Guerrero Ruiz, reports that they insulated one wall of Juan Ramón's workroom with "a cushion made from sacking and esparto grass." A day or two later, the poet complained that the noises were coming through as clear as ever, at least in *his* direction: "for all I know, the neighbor's apartment is much quieter." When the noise became unbearable, he and Zenobia packed up and moved. They did so every few years. "All of our moves have been to flee from noise," he told Guerrero. "We left our apartment on Conde de Aranda because some Cuban ladies were playing the piano and dancing in the apartment upstairs." And there were problems with a cricket; two or three crickets. On the balcony of the apartment next door, a few feet from Juan Ramón's worktable, a little boy and his sister had hung a cricket cage. Juan Ramón complained politely—in his beautiful, nearly illegible script—to their father, an architect, the Count of Manila. All very nice. The Count answered in a poem. He could understand very little of Juan Ramón's "indecipherable logoglypics," but had deciphered the word *grillo*. He was pleased to inform him that the latter had escaped that very night from its tiny prison. Juan Ramón consoled the girl with a doll and the boy with some books, and the Count sent the poet and Zenobia a basket of red carnations.

"And we moved from our apartment at Lista, 8 because one of our neighbors made our lives impossible," he continues. "Velázquez, 96 was ruined when they brought together two trolley lines under our window." For Juan Ramón each move meant packing up thousands of pages of work in progress and falling further behind in his revision.

Outer silence—noiselessness—was nowhere to be found, and he tried to build inner resistance, and tell himself that a little noise was a good thing. "Better than the deserted, absolute backwaters of silence, a warning fence of distant, diffuse human noise." We need noise in order to create, he said; where it doesn't exist, "we will 'make it,' or imagine it." "Without noise I go swimming, flying, jumping over things; with noise, limping and bumping and stumbling into them. But both possibilities are good ..."

— ❄ —

### The Real Cricket

What anguish, that single cricket from that singularly strange month of June (deep and concave June), right there above my open window, nibbling into my solitude like a jingle bell in the inner center of my inner ear! My reverie shaded off into an infinite nightmare, into the whole black sky of summer: into the monotonous pounding of raindrops; leaden stars in an eternity of shadow; immense ocean of black boot polish rippling into one brief and terrible wave that left me choking and gasping for air at each rhythmic blow. The entire concentrated world bearing down on my auditory brain, holding me and yanking me by the head... until I could stand it no longer, and asked Honorio Igelmo, the concierge's son, master of the real cricket, if he would sell it to me. I told him I would give him five pesetas or ten or twenty-five or whatever he wanted, with the idea of carrying the steely, dark little animal to the park and finding a new home for it, far away, in some grassy spot.

The little boy stared at me with enormous eyes that reminded me of two big melancholy, deeply and sadly singing crickets, and I wondered if my question had caused him pain.

No, it hadn't. There was a god of silence and he was watching over me that day.

"For twenty-five pesetas," said the little Castilian, "I'll bring the gentleman five of the best crickets he can imagine!"

## Work

Space, time, solitude, silence.
You find in solitude only what you take to it.

## They keep quiet

Better to be quiet than to speak; to dream than to be quiet; to read than to dream or think. When we read, silence itself grows quiet, and we can think or dream in company.

## Ring

Silence makes everything fit. It is the great gold ring.

Unity is the noble daughter of silence; dispersion, the crazy stepchild of noise.

Noise shatters my day and brain into a thousand little pieces that cannot be glued.

In silence I can have suspended—suspended in the instant—my entire day and even my entire life, in full synthesis. In noise I can only suspend the instant.

Silence is the fountain of time.

Deaf, no; I need to hear the silence.

## Everything makes no sound

There are days when life becomes concave. How things resound in her—the yapping of dogs, the trumpeting of orders, the screams of children, the chirping of birds, the sighs of women!

Other days it becomes convex, and nothing makes a sound at all. Or rather, everything makes no sound." And then, how terrifyingly deaf my life is!

How will the deaf man see the sunset?

When I create, outer noise doesn't bother me, because there is a sort of involuntary concentration like that of dream; but revising and purifying something calls for voluntary abstraction, and it is impossible to avoid the nuisances of one's surroundings.

## Silence and time

Silence does not waste its time, it fills it. Yes. And the one thing that fills time is silence. So, time shared with noise is time lost. But silence conquers time, puts it back together, and makes it whole.

The whole day wandering around the house looking for a place for my thought!

The reason I was so irritated by noise is because it made me move into the next day to enjoy my work and my life, and I let the divine todays go by like so many naked women

I could have possessed but didn't.

In Spain, people wring noise out of just about anything; you could almost say that things are valued only for the noise they make.

Silence fills time and space to its own measure. Noise, which is always small no matter how large it seems, limits them.

## Poetry

Listen to the song of the cricket. First ingenuous, vacillating; later, rhetorical and easy; still later, at midnight, pure, contained, serene, intense, forgetting what it is and what it sings with and where it is; like a star, like a star in the water.

Noise: multiple thorn defending who knows what eternal, virgin rose, immense and invisible.

Who—or What—is it that is using noise to defend itself from analysis?

With noise I can't see.

Noise, how it complicates everything. What a bothersome guest, so sloppy, tangible, dirty, such a fool.

## Like stones

This noise places words in my path like boulders. And somewhere out there, existent and evident, waiting for me, is the great level paradise of silence.

O noises who do nothing to disturb the silence! Noises like thoughts, like meditations, like a huge force of concentration in us, noises who seem to be listening to yourselves, cloaked in your abstraction, in faded outline! Noises like the verses of a poet, which hardly make any sound along the edge, with all the sound at the center; welcome, pleasant noises I need and love: slow tolling of a bell, wandering little bird, falling beads of water.

### Silence and light

Hearing silence and seeing shadow, our life is more luminous and expressive and dwells more within the eternal—I mean, within the sufficient.

When it is noisy, don't sing: draw or sculpt your thought.

When a noise breaks into your silence, make it immediately a natural part of it.

In our successive search for creative silence, we always find new noise, successive noise. (And when there is none, we will want it and hunt it down. We will "make" it so as to struggle with it... and master it?)

So many wasted silences in life!

# The Present

---·※·---

*La eternidad está, nada más, en el presente.*
*Quien "tiene" el presente, tiene la eternidad.*

—JRJ

---·※·---

IT BARELY EXISTS, it pauses for no one, but it is *there* that we must work, defeating what Juan Ramón calls nostalgia—the longing to be somewhere else in time—and holding fast to the present. But who can grab its mane? We reach for it and tumble into the past or future. For Juan Ramón work is a way to ripen the hours, to make them heavier, and to invite the present to linger. Hold the present with your work, and your work will last a long time.

"Almost all that we can be said to enjoy," wrote Samuel Johnson, "is past or future: the present is in perpetual motion, leaves us as soon as it arrives, ceases to be present before its presence is well perceived, and is only known to have existed by the effects which it leaves behind." Juan Ramón makes it a matter of grammar:

> We have been, we will be.
> Yes. But we never are!

He yearns, always, for perfect—for godlike!—concentration. He wants to *be*, thanks to his work. He wants to be present to his work and in his work, and wants to have all of his work fully present before him (see "Revision"). Noise, remorse, worries about his health distract him from what he is making. Among his aphorisms are stratagems and prayers for creating a quiet place in time—a clearing in the forest—where he can work.

— ❊ —

Care for this day! This day is life, the very essence of life. In its weightless passage are all the reality and variety of your existence: the pleasure of growing, the glory of action, the splendor of beauty.

Yesterday is only a dream and tomorrow only a vision. But this day, well lived, makes each yesterday a dream of happiness and each tomorrow a vision of hope. So care for this day!

*(from the Sanskrit)*

Let us conquer each day with the ideas of each day.

If we take good care of today, today will be a true past and tomorrow we will have its memory.

The past is in the present like the grain in an ear of wheat.

### *How can we be bored?*

There have never been two days, two hours, two minutes, two seconds in which nature, life or we ourselves have been, are, will be the same, one and the same. So how can we be bored?

I have never lived in the present; my life is all memories and hopes.

Let us live each day completely, definitively, as a whole and in its details, just in case.

## Past, Present, Future

The future contains nothing more than the past, it "was" the past. So let us calm down and be happy with our daily present, and detain it as long as we can.

Let us get used to seeing in the present all of the past and all of the future.

How the past clings to the feet of the present so as not to let it reach the future without it!

To console ourselves for this constant nostalgia of the future and the past, let us remember, always, that we are the past of those who will come after us, and the future of those who went before; and besides, we are our own present.

Each day let us sweep away what has passed, in order to form *a* past. That way we will give whatever life we have left—though it be only an hour—eternal breadth.

When you're working on one thing and start to yearn for another, imagine that this thing you're working on would be the one you would yearn for if you were working on the other.

Treat the least significant things you do as though they were permanent, and they will endure.

The good has "only" two instants: "*its*" instant and, a while later, "*its*" eternity.

Eternity is only in the present. Who "has" the present, has eternity.

To embrace all of your work, work much on a little each day.

The only way to live: make each instant definitive.

You get to the past through the future.

Eternal death to the renovated ruins of yesterday!

Let us always place ourselves in the future, as much in the future as we can, so that in our old age the long past will not feel heavier than the brief future.

Time and I are enemies.

To feel no nostalgia for pleasurable past hours; and to open hours of new pleasure in the present!

Let us give ourselves fully, without haste, to everything; for everything—fortunately or not—always ends in haste.

Tie up yesterday, set tomorrow free!

## *Light*

Why this scent of flesh and of the infinite in the calm evening? From what radiant woman does it come to me, like a memory of my future life?

I awoke under the sky,
      poor sunken roof,
black and red from night and dawn
with cobwebs, embers, animals.

Getting up, I arranged it as best I could
and under its faint, ragged blue tent
went slowly to what was mine.
And I called that arrangement my day.

# Memory

*¡Quién tuviera, con una buena memoria, un buen olvido!*

—JRJ

FOR JUAN RAMÓN, one of the secrets of finding happiness both in work and in life lay in striking the right balance between remembering and forgetting. "On the scales of your day," give as much to one as to the other. "Watch for their point of equilibrium."

Work, technique, the moral self, depend upon remembered experience in more ways than anyone can count. And yet it annoyed Jiménez, who longed to live and work within the present, that people think of memory as active, beneficial, and unifying, and of forgetting as memory's passive, lazy "sister."

To remember is to put back together into a unified whole, and to forget seems an involuntary coming apart, a dispersion. But for Juan Ramón, an overactive memory could be an obstacle to creation. "My ideal would be 'to forget and to make.' But I remember and remember and remember, and do not make."

When the "useless past" distracts from the work at hand, memories become—in his words—"the seven plagues of the indolent person." And when the writer dwells in the past, or on work already done, he can lose the uniqueness of the present. The writer who can forget is strong not only because she can forgive herself and others but because more of her working moments seem unprecedented and she is better able to concentrate on the work and the beauty that are before her: "Let us respect forgetting, the marvels of forgetting, which allow us to contemplate, isolated from all else, the uniqueness of the present."

Then, too, a memory sometimes needs to vanish completely in order to reveal all of its poetry.

When we forget, something new is received into the unconscious and held for later, for "forgetting loses nothing." She does not simply keep our treasures but transforms them. How often has forgetfulness stolen away the page we were working on and purged it of all that was not... memorable. Juan Ramón is right: "To forget is to be reborn."

— ❋ —

We are constantly worrying, to the point of desperation, about not being able to remember something.

But whether or not we remember it doesn't really matter. We will forget all that we remember and all that we don't.

The balance in our lives comes from making peace between remembering and forgetting. We should not try to force that peace, but let the two of them work it out for themselves, without our intervention.

(Yes, I tell myself, but that isn't really what happens. The fact is, like traitors, we conquer forgetting, giving a moment's help to memory, helping her overthrow that poor, true king.)

Many mistakenly think of memory as an activity, but not forgetting, as though the latter were not also a reality.

The three faculties of the soul: forgetting, will, and understanding.

Forgetting is almost natural; memory, almost artificial.

Ah, who could be as good at forgetting as remembering!

Memory is the daughter of noise; forgetting, the child of silence.

Forgetting is a virtue; memory, a vice.

Poet: to restrain memory is to conquer. To give in to memories is to be conquered.

The strongest man... the one who forgets the most.

Not to relive with pain even a single hour of the past.

For remorse, there is no consolation.

Let us respect forgetting, the marvels of forgetting, which turns us into isolated contemplatives of a unique present.

### Memory

How sad to carry the treasure of each day (up and down) across the bridge of night (down and up) to the other sun!

if only we were content to leave its mantle in the hands of the past; to look no more at what was; to come face to face, pleasurably naked, with the freedom and joy of the present!

A good system for fooling the past—useless past—is to tell it, "Tomorrow I will remember you..." And the next day, the same. And that way it will wither away without our cruelly killing it, its memories will not be strong enough to keep pace with our hopes, and they will lie behind us, dead in the road.

### As in the sea

In the poetic imagination, as in the sea, there may be zones of forgetting, but nothing is ever lost.

### Her key

Forgetting loses nothing; it stores everything up like treasure. And if we are worthy of memory, she will give us the key to forgetting.

### As nothing contains everything

Forgetting contains memory as nothing contains everything: not in negation or enmity but in unity and affirmation.

To forget is to conquer.

To forget is to come back to life.

# Ideals

*Poesía es todo lo bello que no se puede
esplicar y que no necesita esplicación.*

—J R J

NEAR THE TITLE page of some of his books, Juan Ramón drew a sprig of parsley. He wanted to remind himself and his readers that *el trabajo gustoso*, pleasurable work, is not necessarily for gain. In ancient Greece, in the Nemean Games, as in the ones at Olympia, athletes competed not for bronze, silver, or gold, but for a crown of wild celery—perhaps Juan Ramón thought it was parsley—or wild olive. It was an emblem of his idealism, the "fleeting, maximum" reward for his work.

Juan Ramón was an idealist in at least two senses of the word. First, he believed the poet must capture things in their ideal, perfect form rather than the way they exist in reality. Humanity, he thought, had become too fond of reality, too fond of realism: "life and death are *not* what we read about in the newspapers."

And second, he thought of work—his own work, all work—as a spiritual, rather than a materialistic, pursuit. The poet's job, he thought, is to create an ideal world, and he would have agreed with Sir Philip Sidney, that poetry must draw us "to as high a perfection as our degenerate souls, made worse by their clayey lodgings, can be capable of." What does this mean? Simply that the world, as it exists, cannot satisfy our innate craving for perfection: we need the poet to give us a taste of something better. We are given a "brazen" world and only the poet, ranging freely "within the zodiac of his own wit," gives us a golden one. The poet's "making," in this idealistic vision, is really a "remaking," a deeply original kind of imitation that draws out the best in what lies before him. He departs from flawed, unsatisfying particulars and comes as close as possible to a vision of earthly perfection.

It is this habit of seeing beyond reality into the ideal, into what Juan Ramón liked to call "invisible reality," that makes the poet an inspiration to other "makers"; makes him, in the words of Sidney, "in the most excellent work ...the most excellent workman."

As for the other dimension of idealism, Juan Ramón often spoke of a gardener from Seville who drew his happiness, and his only wages, from the poetry of work...

— ❋ —

### The Sevillian Gardener

In Seville, in the Triana neighborhood, in a lovely garden overlooking the Guadalquivir, on a street—it seems almost too much, but this is true—a street named *Ruiseñor*, Nightingale... From the patio, you could see the sun setting against the cathedral and its tower: fiery rose in the lush dark green. The gardener, a big, refined fellow, used to sell plants and flowers that he cared for, exquisitely, on his balcony. For him, each plant was like a woman or delicate child: together, they were a family of leaves and blossoms. How hard for him to sell them, to let them go, to part with a single one! And this particular spiritual struggle (for he had one every day) was over a pot of hydrangeas.

Some people came to buy it and, after mulling it over and conquering his doubts, he worked out an agreement. He would sell that pot on one condition: that he be allowed to take care of it. Away they went with his hydrangea. For a few days the gardener went to see it at the home of its new owners. He would take off the dead leaves, water it, add or remove a bit of soil, and prop it up better against its little trellis. And before he left he would give instructions: "The way you water it is important...When it's in the sun, put it like this...Be especially careful when it's damp at night..." And so on.

The owners were getting tired of his visits ("All right, all right, you've made your point. We'll see you *next month*..."), and the gardener went to see them less often; or, rather, he went as often but didn't go inside. He would go down the street and gaze at the hydrangea through the grating of the patio. Or he would enter rapidly, a little embarrassed, on some pretext or other: "I found this syringe, and it'll help you water it better," or "I had forgotten about this little wire," and so on. All this in order to see "his" hydrangea.

And finally one day he appeared, renewed and resolute. "If you don't want me to come take care of it, you can tell me how much you want for it, and I'll take it home with me this very moment." Into his arms he took the big blue flowerpot with the pink hydrangea and carried it off like a little girl.

The great tree of truth has its roots in the earth and its fruits in the sky.

Since the fruits are ours, how we miss them!

## Realm of the idea

Could anything be more satisfying than to restore to the realm of the idea what reality has degraded?

## Invisible realities

Invisible realities are what I want, where invention can rest its wing. Its arm and leg are already resting on the visible.

For me, the impossible is like the star hidden in the day, and it exists like the sure star of night.

What is glimpsed is more visible and lasts longer than what is seen.

The art of appearances is lovelier than the art of realities.

There are no better draftsmen than dust and shadow.

I would like to peer over the edge of the horizon. There, down deep, waiting for me to fall—to my death?—is what I am yearning for.

Why shouldn't I love, adore, feel reverence for my work if it is the most enduring and loveliest body I can possibly make for my soul?

I see her everywhere. I understand her, but she doesn't reveal herself to me. Perhaps it is simply that I can't find her name.

A poet is merely a discontented person who transforms the world according to his whim—who changes for himself and others the appearance of the creation.

Poetry is like a bird that comes in a moment of rapture from the heavens into the heart. What takes skill is knowing how to send it from the heart back into the heavens.

Food, drink, after-dinner conversation, sex, anything that can be realized and completely enjoyed in the act: none of this is for poetry. For prose, maybe, especially the novel. Poetry is for whatever cannot be *had*; this is the way it works and its particular charm.

Poetry is all beauty that cannot be explained and needs no explanation.

In poetry what can be resolved in a circle is never everything. By contrast, what remains half resolved on a difficult middle ground, is always a path.

Poetry that doesn't take hold, that isn't contagious, no matter how good it is, is useless.

Poetry is further from the seeker than god[1] is from the mystic or truth is from the philosopher.

[1] I write 'god' with a small letter the way I write father and mother, glory and sea, earth, heaven, etc. And woman. It is not irreverence but neither is it reverence. It isn't fear; it is—with a small letter—love.  JRJ

---  ❋  ---

# Nature

*Raíces; pero que las alas arraiguen y las raíces vuelen.*
—JRJ

---  ❋  ---

THE POET CALLS himself a "maker" and from earliest times has compared his powers of making not only to those of nature but also, without blushing, to those of the divinity, the "Maker of that maker." Sidney presses the point in his *Apology*. Surely, he writes, it is "not too saucy a comparison" to "balance the highest point of man's wit with the efficacy of nature." In so doing, the poet

> give[s] right honor to the heavenly Maker of that maker, who having made man to His own likeness, set him beyond and over all the works of that second nature, [for] our erected wit maketh us know what perfection is, and yet our infected will keepeth us from reaching unto it.

For the poet—Sidney, Emerson, Rilke, Keats—the book of nature is (in Juan Ramón's words) "an inexhaustible source of spiritual norms." Nature tells him what and when and how to make. It gives him norms that bear on his way of life and manner of work and serve as imaginary touchstones for the verbal objects he creates. Emerson tells us of the poet's intuition that

> [his] poems are a corrupt version of some text in nature, with which they ought to be made to tally. A rhyme in one of our sonnets should not be less pleasing than the iterated nodes of a sea-shell, or the resembling difference of a group of flowers. The pairing of the birds is an idyll, not tedious as our idylls are; a tempest is a rough ode, without false-hood or rant …why should not the symmetry and truth that modulate these, glide into our spirits and we participate the invention of nature?

Juan Ramón is more succinct:

> No matter how short, a line of verse is always longer than a seed; no matter how long, shorter than the tail of a mouse.

To compare human work to the quiet, rhythmic work of nature, from the growth of an oak tree to the formation of a star or pinecone is another way to meditate on perfection. How, Juan Ramón wondered, does one follow nature toward perfection?

> If we look at a star, it seems perfect at each moment: an enchanting, mysterious star. But it is successive, it is always making itself, always traveling toward itself, toward its pos-sibility or impossibility…

This is one of the "spiritual norms" he derived from the natural world. It was an idea of "successiveness," of beauty in progress, that consoled him for the imperfections in his own work. He taught himself to think of his work as star, desert, ocean, sky: images of constant change. Nature, too, is always revising, always correcting itself, preparing a new version, and as it does so, always suggesting the right qualities—firmness or delicacy, speed or slowness—for the work at hand. Out walking, in the cool morning

> Rodin plucks a mushroom, delighted, and shows it to Madame Rodin ..."Look," he says excitedly, and that takes but a single night! In one night all these are made, all these lamellas. That is good work.

It is probably more difficult now than it was in Keats's day, or Emerson's or even Rodin's or Juan Ramón's, to find lessons about work in the book of nature. For nature has become too much *ours*, and can no longer be the "something else"—the book written by someone else—that we can learn from. We are too involved in it to draw lessons from it. Juan Ramón, for whom rhythm was one of the deepest secrets of poetry and work, could see, even in the 1940s, that the rhythms of nature were becoming human:

> What do I care about three annual crops of California apples, which taste like wood, when I have another Spanish apple, which takes a year to develop its juices?

Writers on bioethics sometimes remind their readers, sensibly, that the "us and it" distinction is false: that man, too, forms part of a "community of living things." But, in an age when every prodigy seems attributable to human intervention, the natural world seems more a reflection of our work rather than a norm for it.

We can remember, though, that the idea of nature has always been an imaginative construct (Juan Ramón's "nature" was the Retiro, in Madrid); that it has sprung from the minds of poets; and that, even in Emerson's day, it was an elusive part of reality. Nature is always "elsewhere," he wrote.

> What splendid distance, what recesses of ineffable pomp and loveliness in the sunset! But who can go where they are, or lay his hand or plant his foot thereon? Off they fall from the round world forever and ever.

Nature is *still* elsewhere. We need it for our work, but must work a little harder to evoke it. It is not outside us but within, this idea of pristine nature—the idea of a process that is not ours but can provide norms and images for the work of writing. Within us, still, is an idea of all that is *not* us: the breeze, a bird, the constellations ("golden summits of the dark"), as in Juan Ramón's proud credo of poetic freedom:

> This is my life, the one above,
> the one of pure breeze,
> the last bird,
> the golden summits of the dark!

> This is my freedom: to smell the rose,
> slice the cold water with my crazy hand,
> strip the poplar grove,
> and steal from the sun its eternal light!

— ✳ —

### *Take root and fly*

Roots and wings. But let the wings take root and the roots take flight.

### *Present order*

In great mother nature, the primitive mountain and the little goldfinch, the recent violet and the centenary pine, the largest and smallest of things, the superficial and the profound, live together and successively in the present order without opposition of time or space. And yet, all has its time and its place.

That is the way I would like my own bible to be; I mean, that is the way I would like to be in my book.

Observe natural phenomena and you will find in them an inexhaustible source of spiritual norms.

The sea, full of animal, vegetable, and mineral detritus and the detritus of gods, and where we nonetheless bathe in pure water, is an excellent norm for everything else in our lives.

I met someone who had so forgotten clear water that he thought it was a cosmetic.

I would like my verses to give the impression of natural phenomena; to be as eternal (and definitive) as a sunset, as flowing water, as the fantasies of the moon on cloudy nights.... I would like them to be a force of nature, a weak one—isn't Blue Vervain strong when it takes root under a boulder?—constant and renewed. I would like criticism to have nothing to do with my verses. I would like them to suspend the soul, as though they were a fountain of ideas, of colors, of sensations... and as though no one had written them.

As long as I live, my writing will change every time I read it. Not that I force it; the writing itself comes to me changed, I can't help it. My life is to relive what I did 50 years ago, 40, 30, 20, 10, 1 year, one day, one hour ago. I have often said that I feel like a sea in movement where the same waves are constantly changing.

This isn't a literary technique. It is some sort of palpable transformation in nature, or in me. It is a different idea of poetry. It makes sense for something to get better each time it is relived. Critics need not look for a better explanation than this. I am like nature. Can't help it.

## The art of work

O critic of my being, is there anything more artificial, more artistic than the work of water and earth, fire and air? Unconscious nature works only with art, the art of work, which she never enunciates but only learns, deaf and dumb, one century after another, in the dark. And it is we who call ourselves men who can consciously appreciate the depth of that art.

What deceives man, in his appreciation, is that the artificial work of nature is given to him already "done," and he has grown accustomed to this age-old fact, and thus thinks it "natural" and effortless. Whereas he has to do his own work in a hurry and with critical consciousness …

People say "go to nature" and "leave your books." But one shouldn't go to books only to see nature copied (in books it is a mere pretext) but to see art, which is no less "natural" than nature.

### Like nature

Things are praised for being "imperfect, like nature." But we shouldn't forget that nature is imperfect because unconscious. If it were conscious, it would be perfect.

When we evoke the rose as an example of simplicity, we don't usually think of the centuries nature took to create it.

To those who ask why we often make things that are delicate and subtle, etc.—"useless" things—I reply that nature provides me with an example.

What crystallization, what iridescence, what harmonies are stylized by nature! And within ourselves, the eyes, hands, lips, fingers, the most expressive parts of us, aren't they prodigies of refinement and subtlety?

So why must the rough be more "human" than the refined, as rough people think? And why add that these exquisite things are artificial? Is a butterfly artificial? A seashell, a tiny wildflower? Are mountains any more natural than these? And why say a wildflower is natural and it is not natural or delicate to copy it the way it is?

Doesn't a meteor have the same beauty as a mountain? In the day, I prefer the fugitive almost invisible meteor; at night, the almost invisible mountain.

I don't know why it should it be more beautiful, more meritorious to make the word a cobblestone than to make it a flame. Because the flame goes away and the stone endures? No. The cobblestone can obstruct, and the flame knows how to hide.

The idea that granite is more consistent and solid than a bee! But beauty isn't measured with the fist. It is measured with the strength of our awareness.

All the world is naked and it creates man naked. Ay! Only man gets dressed, and wants to dress the world!

A sense of the artificially immense is depriving the world of its sense of the naturally large.
Artificial immensity is only the sum of artificial smallness; the naturally large includes the naturally small, but is not its sum.

Of all trees, the eternal green pine. Of all landscapes, red stone against a blue sky, with white clouds. (And the sea; or better, the illusion of the sea.)

"Natural" art. Aesthetic creation shouldn't be forced with any stimulus, either physical or intellectual (coffee, places, readings, tobacco, wine, travel, the hour); it should be the spontaneous issue of clear, current life.

## My writing

I imagine my writing as a true sea, because it is made from innumerable waves; as a true sky, because it is made from innumerable stars; as a true desert, because it is made from innumerable grains of sand.

And like the sky, the sea, the desert, it is always in motion and in change.

I think that the most perfect formal and spiral norm for the artist—light, idea, color, matter, feeling—is the star.

To die uncorrupted, like the day and the night.

A diamond with the cool freshness of grass.

Violet steel.

If you cannot be gold, be silver. But not silver with gold plate.

## Immense rose

I imagine our world as an immense, total rose of fire, stone, water and air, carrying in its bosom forms of surprising, unique, absolute beauty.

The rose, is it geometrical?

How alien to their meaning and to their name: the rose and the nightingale!

### Barnyard fowl

When you learn of someone who speaks badly about the nightingale, go take a look. You will surely find a starling or a hen.

### And only one

When we used to offer flowers to my mother, she would always answer, "A wild rose, and only one."

I have never forgotten that, nor will I ever. It is my norm.

Two roses are two; four, four; seven, seven. Many, one.

For me the best image of the infinite is in the tiny seed.

> White cloud:
> broken wing (whose?)
> unable to arrive (where?)

No matter how much men discover, they will never make it possible for us to leave this earth of ours. So let us think that here we have everything, that here we will come to an end and be indefinitely reborn; and let us, the living and the dead, feel immense affection for this poor, round world of ours: our father, son, daughter, brother, lover.

---

# Instinct

*Si te dan papel rayado, escribe de través;*
*si atravesado, del derecho.*

—JRJ

---

SOONER OR LATER any poetics of work tries to mediate between two inner forces that govern creation, sometimes imagined as working in synchrony and sometimes as separate phases in the creative process. In Juan Ramón those two forces are often imagined as "instinct and intelligence." Other poets have spoken of different dichotomies: the conscious and the unconscious, feeling and thinking, inspiration and imagination, the Apollonian and the Dionysian, the angel and the duende. For Juan Ramón, perfect work places those forces—whatever their names— in equilibrium. There can be no creative work without instinct, but a wholly instinctive artist would be, for him, a wholly irresponsible one.

In accounts of poetic creation, one of the two is usually given special privileges. "The talk of inspiration is sheer nonsense," William Morris once wrote. "There is no such thing. It is a mere matter of craftsmanship." Poe explaining how he composed "The Raven," or Valéry lecturing ironically on the making of his *Cimitière marin*, chose to present creation as a series of deliberate choices, a purely voluntary exercise in

which scarcely anything is left to chance. What Poe set out
to prove was that "no one point in [the] composition [of his
poem] is referable either to accident or intuition—that the
work proceeded, step by step, to its completion with the precision and rigid consequences of a mathematical problem."
A writer weighs the pros and cons of a rhythm, genre, mood,
form, word, and comes to a "rational" solution. Valéry:

> I seek a word (says the poet) a word which is
> feminine,
> has two syllables,
> contains p or f,
> ends in a mute vowel ...

But perhaps those deliberations came along after the fact?
First Chance, then Choice, limping along behind. How
strong, how resistant to chance, is intelligence, anyway? García Lorca warned that "intelligence is often the enemy of
poetry, because it limits too much, and it elevates the poet
to a sharp-edged throne where he forgets that ants could eat
him or that a great arsenic lobster could fall on his head."

In Juan Ramón's poetics, as in Lorca's (both were Roman-
tics), it is instinct that gets special treatment. Juan Ramón
isn't entirely sure what instinct *is*, and he knows that it is not
always the enemy of intelligence: some intelligent people are
"instinctively" so. On the whole, though, he wants to make
the "dirty owl" of intelligence more attentive to instinct,
more respectful, more patient with its finds; teach intelligence to be a little more humble, both in work and in daily
life. For in life, too, we can transform instinct, "through
education and culture, into superior insight." As for "blind

intelligence," when it is not led by instinct, it does not "serve to guide a man through his world, but can only help him understand it." Instinct delivers the goods—a line of poetry, for example—"and intelligence must work hard to comprehend it," work hard not to laugh enviously or coax that line into looking normal. As always, as happens with his struggle to balance memory and forgetting, for Juan Ramón instinct and intelligence must work together: when instinct opens up like a strange plant, intelligence knows where to place it and what to feed it.

Instinct guides work, but is also summoned by work: by concentration, receptivity, and the desire for perfection. Rilke writes that Rodin's concentration was so prodigious

> that he shrugs off the imputation of inspiration and claims that there is no such thing—no inspiration, but rather only labor—[and] then one suddenly comprehends that to this creator receptivity has become so continuous that he no longer feels its coming, because it is no longer ever absent.

— ❊ —

...Inspiration is like a momentary spark from a more perfect—and perhaps more enduring—life. It is like a window of the soul open to a possible existence, an equanimous life which exists in theory, and which we could get to in the depths of our spirit.

I believe in inspiration, but don't trust it very much.

Life gets along well with the unconscious. But as soon

as we confront her with our thought, oh how—with how many weapons: noise, cold, pain, heat—she defends herself!

So that my whole me can be content with my work, I need my conscious half to refine, measure, define, and fix what my subconscious has created.

### The work

If my work were to make itself, without any effort on my part, I would like it very little ; if I were to make it alone, without any will on *its* part, I would like it even less.

There are men whose intelligence can be called instinct, and other, irrational ones, whose instinct can be called intelligence (supposing that instinct and intelligence are but degrees of a single power.)

Instinct, where is the strength, the wisdom, the magic that can isolate you?

How many shy little things realized by intuition have been explained, sanctioned condescendingly by jealous intelligence?

In art and letters I will always be against two things: the strictly cerebral and the monstrous and instinctive.

### She knows how to get even

Intelligence usually dominates instinct. But instinct,

which is older than intelligence and also younger—for it
is permanent—knows how to get even. How few times
the dirty owl of intelligence escapes from instinct's terrible,
clean, sharp beak! And yet, how few times Venus comes
completely out of the sea, virgin and pure, in her own special
manner.

### And the ordinary word

Rare intuition and the ordinary word: the greatest beauty.

There is a place within us that can be reached by intelligence. But there is a deeper place that only the spirit can
get to. And that is why those who are "merely completely
intelligent"—in science or art, verse or prose—always seem
like spies.

### More than a little

Let our intelligence keep an eye on our instinct. But let
us give that child enough freedom to do a little—more than
a little—of what it wants.

### To comprehend it

Intelligence isn't there to guide instinct, but to comprehend it.

### And gain much

Our instinct is constantly correcting us. And if we follow

its correction, after having thought about it, we will lose nothing and gain much.

People think reflection destroys the work that is felt. No, no: feeling knows how to defend herself from thought, like a woman from a man, keeping him where he belongs.

Feel ideas acutely, and meditate slowly on feeling.

You needn't feel ashamed your worst instinct... Lead it like a blind man inside you, tame it like a beast, love it as you would an inferior self.

The great works of others are now my tuning forks.

If they give you lined paper, write the other way...

*And*

Caprice and crucible.

---— ✴ ——---

# Dream

*Hay que prolongar el ensueño hasta más allá del ocaso.*

—JRJ

---— ✴ ——---

IN DREAM AND reverie work lies fallow. The will to finish, to solve a problem, is suspended. Something that is not the will takes over, juxtaposing images that would not have come together during waking hours And often, passively, something emerges into the conscious mind—though not exactly a solution or even an idea. In his dreams, Juan Ramón was aware only of "colors, planes, lights, positions in time and space," or the vague feeling of something having happened:

> I have a feeling that my boat
> has struck, down there in the depths,
> against a great thing. And nothing
> happens! Nothing... Silence... Waves...
>
> Nothing happens! Or has everything happened,
> and we are standing now, quietly, in the new life?
>
> (TRANSLATED BY ROBERT BLY)

Poems and aphorisms about dreams and daydreams are

everywhere in Juan Ramón's work, and he regards dreams with deep reverence, and always from a certain distance.

> Power who use me, like a sleepwalking medium, for your mysterious communications, I must conquer you, yes, and know what it is you are saying, what you make me say when you possess me; I must know what it is I say, some day.

For him, dreams are not a way of discovering information about his work or about himself. As he bends over the water, he sees beyond his own distorted reflection into depths that have apparently nothing to do with him at all. Dreams attract him, as nature does, precisely because they are *not him*, because they allow him a glimpse of another order of things. He is doubtful he can capture the language of dreams in his writing, and although he speaks often of the pleasures of dreaming, few of his poems are the narration of actual dreams, and he knows that there are dream strata, "below our lives and above our deaths," which neither the psychologist or the poet will ever get at. Following a long tradition of Spanish poets—the best known is Calderón de la Barca—he affirms that, when the play is over, what is "lived" is indistinguishable from what is "dreamt." Idealists like Juan Ramón can never easily decide which of these two halves of our lives is the "real" one. Some of his poems make us feel that we are flying at night, upside down, unable to know whether those lights are coming from the stars or from an earthly city. In others, there is a jolt when he returns to the "fool's gold" of day.

He believes firmly in the restorative power of dreams: they are the "madness" that keeps us sane; the poetry that chastens our reality and purifies what happened the day before. From the verge of his dream he can hear his work beckoning: "the poem calls to me, like love, from its place." In the morning, in the "already blue of the sky," he walks along an imaginary beach, looking for what has been left there by the tides of dream. He picks up "only what glows in the dawn," and ignores the driftwood fondled by surrealists. The notion of "automatic writing"— dictation taken down from dream—runs counter to his notion of the poet as "above all, responsible." If there is a lesson for work to be drawn from his thoughts on dreaming, it is this: "dream toward the spirit" and not toward reality, and let your dreams alone. They are the part of you that, happily, you cannot control. They are all that is not your work. By themselves, uncoerced, they will remind you of your limits, carry you outside them, and refresh you in your daily labor.

— ※ —

Thought that can't get through the fence at night... leave it in the henhouse of evening.

I want to look at things, but I only see through them.

Sometimes my daydreams follow one another so closely and abundantly that I think I am bleeding to death.

Prolong your reverie beyond the sunset.

### Harbor

When we're asleep, our body
is the anchor
our soul leaves
on the seabed of our life.

### My hand deep inside you

Riches of night, how many secrets pulled from you, how many yet to take, though none of them is your secret or mine, night!

What unspeakable pleasure, to plunge my hand deep inside, stirring your stars!

And... luminous touch of other hands searching for your treasures!

I can pluck more from dream than from life, for dream is like a better life, whose roses I would like to plant in my reality.

...In our dreams memory makes us "sane with blackness," and this seems a natural state for us: more natural, at least, than "crazy with light."

Let us dream whatever we want, for when life and dream are gone, a thing lived is no better than a thing dreamt.

I sing my dreams to sleep like a mother singing to her crying children.

Try to balance the sadness of a lost dream or lost idea with the joy of some work that has been realized.

Rapid creation, as in dream.

Not to dream? But dream is the prelude, the mainspring of action; and the best, most beautiful action is the one dreamt of!

I dreamt I was dead and that, dead, I was dreaming that I was coming back to life and could not. And I dreamt that dream would be eternal.

## Just as I was finding

What a shame to awaken now, just as I was finding in the life of dream what I had lost in the dream of life.

How very sad! Last night I learned the origin of things and was at the center of the secret of the universe. I was the possessor of all the highest reasons for our existence, and *now what*? The fiery nightmare of "life," the tragic, ugly sun of people hawking their wares in nasal voices and beating their carpets.

How tired my whole body feels, abandoned by its royal guest. And how long it takes, poor thing, to resign itself to the "natural" blood pressure that propels it once again toward the false—the pressure wide-awake doctors call "normal," felt in one's pulse and reflexes: signs that vile man has been tossed out of timeless dream into the teeming waiting room of three o'clock...!

In the morning, like a gardener, I sweep up the fallen leaves of my dreams.

Every morning when I go to the beach of yesterday, I pick up only what has been purified at night by the sea, only what glows in the dawn.

Awakenings are usually sad, for life catches us without warning, after the treasures of dream ...And so morning is something like a ruin, bankrupcy. Thought and light begin adapting to one another, and we get that miserable fictitious structure called "day," fool's gold. Simulacrum of a great, beautiful life that must exist someplace else...

### Foreseen stopping place

Dream is the atmosphere of superior reality from which we emerge molded and modeled every morning for a new physical and moral impulse: the true lodging along our magical road, a stopping place foreseen, day after day, on the way to our final destination.

### Catch it by surprise

If we could catch it by surprise, the word from our dreams could be our best and truest.

### Nocturnal language

The word of dream, nocturnal language, is other than itself. To put it differently: when we awake, what we usually believe we were saying in our dreams isn't usually what we were saying, even if, out of haste, indifference, boredom, or forgetfulness, it seems to be the same and satisfies us.

In the state between sleep and wake, just before we awaken, on the very border of ourselves, standing on the bank, as though changing languages at the frontier, we do a subconscious or unconscious translation of the world of dream: a strange, subtle exchange which differs from itself as greatly as the nude of our dream differs in color, touch, charm and mystery differs from the nude of reality.

They are two and they are one. Two in one, as we ourselves are.

### Sleepless

Night goes away, black bull (dense flesh of mourning, fright, and mystery) that has bellowed terrible and immense, making the fallen sweat with fear, and day comes, fresh child asking trust, love and laughter (child who, far away, in the hidden places where beginnings meet endings, has played for a moment on I know not what prairie of light and shadow with the bull that was fleeing.)

### Above and below our death

The dreams we dream are deposited in the depths of our being, as in the successive levels of a mine. The first level can be found easily when we awaken: light dreams, a blanket of foam, fleeting sadness or happiness. It takes more effort to find the second one, under its thick fur. Perhaps sometime we will find the third one, coming upon it by surprise. The fourth... has a double or quadruple layer... And suddenly there is another level that we can't even glimpse, deep down in its lair, without any relation to us at all.

We live and die at one, two, three meters below "our earth." In "our earth" everything that is "ours" happens to us, even "our" dreams. Somebody or something has placed that final level at his or its own level, that stratum which we will never be able to excavate and which remains, always, beneath our life and above our death ...

I have dreamt my life and lived my dream.

### [Prayer]

O dream, you who are the truth, or a simulacrum of the truth; who give us strength to return to falsehood and who are like a key to each day of the future; who have no balance, but balance the senses and the will; O madness who keep us sane and poetry who make our reality: brush me with your big sweet wings; open my eyes inward into myself; quiet the murmuring in my ears; and make me see the light I cannot see and the melody I cannot hear.

---·❋·---

# Death

*Lo malo de la muerte no ha de ser más que la primera noche.*

—JRJ

---·❋·---

WHY DEATH IN a poetics of work? The very thought of it can bring work to a standstill. Juan Ramón's fellow poet Unamuno liked to quote the anonymous Spanish song:

> When I remember I must die,
> I lay my cape on the floor
> and get my fill of sleep.

But the thought of death can also be a spur to creation. The approach of evening and night alters the tempo and rhythm of work, and the struggle to produce enduring work is a consolation for, and distraction from, and a vivid protest against, mortality and anonymity.

### THE WORK

> Yes, just for a little while!
> And yet, since each minute
> can be an eternity,
> what a unique little while!

Good work offers consolation for the brevity of life. Unamuno insists, "Work is the only *practical* consolation we have
for being born."

Juan Ramón was always worrying—always consulting
his doctors—about whether he would have enough time
to revise, "definitively" arrange, and publish the best he had
written. Ever more often, he conjured up his death, remind-
ing himself, his wife Zenobia, and his friends and enemies,
that he had been born with a weak heart and cursing its
dysrhythmia for interrupting the flow of his daily labor. The
thought of death has special meaning for those like him who
conceive of their work not as a series of tasks—these can
be left to others—but as a whole. In the evening he would
often measure the time he thought he had left against the
work that remained:

> All my work is well organized now. Not in vain have I
> worked my whole life, without missing a single day, and if
> I could just have another ten years and could just leave my
> work finished, I wouldn't mind having it placed beside that
> of anyone else from any period, from any country. But one
> of these days an artery pops, and it's all over. I would like to
> work until I'm sixty, at least: I think one can still work fully
> at sixty: more than that, I don't know…And so my norm
> these days is to bring things to completion.

It was April 1934. He lived another twenty-four years, and
died at age seventy-seven. Among the hundred thousand
manuscript pages in the archives are the outlines of many
unpublished books—memos to posterity—from which the

late Antonio Sánchez Romeralo, Mercedes Juliá, María Estela Harretche, Javier Blasco, and many other scholars have pieced together his unfinished quilt: his *Obra*.

For him, to remember death was also to remember the "eternity" he wanted for his work: "I think so much about death because I know that when I am dead, I am going to live more than I did when alive." Death, he thought, would complete him, closing the circle—the "orbit" or "zero"—of his life.

## LIGHT AND SHADOW

I will not be me, death, until you come together with my life and bring me to completion; not until my half of light is closed with my half of shadow and I can be eternal balance in the mind of the world: at times, the half that is radiant, and at times the half that is oblivion...

One of Juan Ramón's favorite ploys, so that the thought of death would neither stop him in his tracks, or make his work unbearable, was to treat death as a familiar presence. Centuries earlier, Francisco de Quevedo –a prodigious worker terrified by death—calmed himself in the same way, with the thought that death is already "inside" us, already part of us even before we leave the womb:

Before it learns to walk the foot is spurring
down the road to death.

Life, in Quevedo's nihilistic equation, is "living death." If it *is* at all, it is a "nothing that, being, is little, and will be nothing." Death isn't something that comes from afar, from someplace outside, out of the future or the past; it is already here. Quevedo came to imagine himself as a "present succession of the dead." Entombed within him were the child, the youth, the man he had once been: an image to which Juan Ramón returns in one of his aphorisms. He feels like "a sepulcher full of all my dead." But Juan Ramón treats death more tenderly and intimately and humorously than Quevedo, or Lorca with his *duende* (for Juan Ramón, Lorca's *duende* "has an unhealthy odor of plumbing.") What was there to fear from such a quiet, familiar presence?

> What happens to music
> when it ceases to sound,
> to a breeze that ceases to flutter,
> to a light that ceases to burn?
>
> Death, tell me, what are you but silence,
> calm, and shadow?

— ❊ —

All my life, in every place, every day, in every light and color; asleep and awake, happy and sad, poor and rich, I have felt death by my side. I'm beginning to think that she likes having me as a living friend.

What an obsession with death! Perhaps the earth seems to be waiting for me, sadly, as for a prodigal son.

Why are the dead so heavy? Is it because when we are

alive the spirit lifts us with the luminous pull of the heavens? Is it because flesh without soul is only collapse and ruin? Ah, the heaviness of the dead!

## DEATH
### (MOTHERS)

At times I love in my mother
an unknown eternal mother
who has lived for a long time
—mother of grandmothers of grandmothers—
in some distant nothing; who watches me
with anxious eyes,
and comes closer, closer ...

The yawn: anticipation of the tomb! Taste of the earth of the dead, entering the gut!

What does death matter if, in life and in work, we have conquered it day after day: if we have gone beyond it in our thoughts and our hearts?

### Between two eternities

Why this fear of death if, from the infinite origin of the world until our birth, we were in death so pleasantly, and have such lovely memories of what went before our accidental, momentary existence between one eternity and another?

Perhaps this momentary life of ours is only the light that divides our infinite origin from our infinite end?

To die, what we call dying, is not to die but only to die

another time.

Every morning we emerge from the grave.

> Ah, sleep,
> how we learn in you to die!
> With what magisterial beauty
> you lead us (through gardens
> that seem more and more ours)
> to the great knowledge of the dark!

I am nothing more than a sepulcher full of all my dead; and my tomb will simply be another me.

To live is nothing more than to come here to die, to be what we were before being born, but with apprenticeship, experience, knowledge of cause, and perhaps with will.

The only bad part of death must be the first night.

Dear wife, to return to nothing will be like going back to our little house after a short or a long trip through this foreign life.

As with life, one is dead for a certain period only. We might say that death lasts no longer than life. After seventy or eighty years of earth, we are no longer dead, just as we are no longer alive after seventy or eighty years of life.

Death is no longer than life. 10 years of life, 10 years of death; 30, 30; 80, 80.

First nonbeing; then birth; then life; then death; then nonbeing.

"To be" dead is "to be." Being. Life.

Life kills nonbeing; death kills life; nonbeing kills death. To be born, live die. Three airy episodes in nonbeing.

### The dead man

Remember me! I have only the life you give me!

I think so much about death because I know that when I am dead I am going to live more than I did when alive.

### Orbits, zeros, graves

Our orbit is a zero: a line and a void. And all we do is draw that zero each minute, hour, day, week, month, year. If we stumble, the zero is a grave.

If today I am seventy years old, how many zeros have I drawn around the zero of the sun? Into how many graves have I stumbled?

All of space is full of orbits, zeros, and the infinite mystery, the immense zero.

Creation: immense zero to be stumbled into, immense grave!

Add it up.

# Writing

*Poesía es lo casi dicho, literatura lo dicho, retórica lo redicho.*
*Lo casi dicho tiene, pues, la primera categoría bella.*

—JRJ

WRITING IS WORK and the record of work, and a way to make ourselves fully conscious of our work. The effort to write and work perfectly is a way of pursuing form and eluding death, the end of form.

Juan Ramón compares writing to love:

> First, the word itself, alone, an island. Next, the blissful joining, as in love, of two words. Later, finally, the whole period, like a world both closed and open ...

He suggests that only what is written slowly and lovingly can last, given the right conditions. He marvels over the frailness of his medium: "Beauty on a sheet of paper! To live even a little, you must elude fire, support the air, escape from water, cheat the earth!" Even if his manuscripts endured, surviving mold and fire and the chaos of war and of life in exile, who would need and remember his writing? Who would take pleasure in it? That thought helped him to dwell in the present, to forget posterity ("Such haste to be eternal!"), and to rejoice in writing for its own sake.

> This or that person says to me, "Why this eagerness, this insistence, this ecstasy over your work?"
> I answer with this delicious poem of Abū Saīd, the Persian: "I asked my beloved, 'Why do you make yourself beautiful?'"
> "To please myself," she answered. "Because there are moments when I am, at the same time, the mirror and the woman looked at and beauty itself; moments when I feel that I am, at the same time, love and the lover and the beloved."

In writing, Juan Ramón tells us, perfection is a matter of equilibrium. He wants to balance brevity and fullness; spontaneity and exactness; the rare word and the common one; the wish to control his own meaning, and the ability to let go and trust the reader.

Two of his ideals are simplicity and freshness. He wants his writing to be succulent as a fruit, right as a seed. "Not a walnut, not an odorless dahlia." He recoils from archaism, rhetoric, padding: all these belong to "literature," and for him, "literature" and "poetry" are at opposite poles of writing. Literature is voluntary and complicated; poetry, instinctive and simple.

Literature is decorative, ingenious, external, because it is created by comparing, commenting, and copying. Literature is translation; poetry, original. Poetry is for deep feelings, literature is for superficial ones. Poetry is instinctive—terse and easy like a fruit or a flower. It comes in one piece. But literature, in its struggle to "incorporate" the external, is "worked over," juxtaposed, Baroque.

These words, from a lecture, allude to, and exemplify, a

tension in his own writing. Juan Ramón struggled, in his own words, with a "Baroque architect with indigestion" who wanted to take over his writing. Among his papers, saved by chance from the "kaleidoscope" of his wastebasket, we find symmetrical "Baroque" fragments like this one:

> Give the women in your life all that you want to, know how to, and can. Accept from them all that they can, know how to, and want to give you. And don't be occupied or preoccupied with what they want, know how to, or can give to others...

Perfect writing, he thought, was otherwise. He liked to think of it as "naked." Poetry can wear sandals, but never shoes. In all perfect writing, the form is there, but it is invisible, "like the current of a river," and the form and accent are one's own.

Unamuno once said that perfect work— whether the work of a shoemaker or that of a civil servant—seems irreplaceable because it is unique. He spoke of work so good that through it the worker makes his own death seem an inconsolable insult, an outrage. The same applies to writing and to the aura of uniqueness known as style. For Juan Ramón style is not a matter of linguistic idiosyncrasy. "Style is not the pen, and not the language." It isn't the "juggling act" of that hateful Baroque architect. To find one's style is to find "the exact, the only expressive path for our being... the unbreakable thread in our living labyrinth. Our inexhaustible and pleasurable current." And this is true of all good work: it is a "path for our being." In the thought of Juan Ramón, writing is an image of work, and work is an image of writing: they are the shadow of the form we leave on the earth.

— ❊ —

First, the word itself, alone, an island. Next, the blissful joining, as in love, of two words. Later, finally, the whole period, like a world both closed and open, containing (within itself, within itself alone) the infinite.

What matters in writing, I think, is that the ordinary word seems to be used for the first time, and the rare one seems ordinary, so that one doesn't stumble over it either, and (as I've often said) no word feels strange or wrong, wherever it is placed...

Defending an "approximate" poetic writer, another half-writer said, "It's just that *we* don't want to find the exact word but the approximate one."

"Yes to both of you," I said, "but the word which is the word which isn't the word, that one too must be found, and found exactly."

### Authentic sonnet

The true sonnet is the one that, being a sonnet in a beautiful way, makes us forget it is a sonnet and remember only that it is beautiful.

In poetry, the word should be so exact that the reader forgets it and only the idea remains: a little like a river that makes us forget the water and remember only the current.

…May my word be the thing itself, newly created by my soul. And may all who do not know them go through me to things; and all who forget them go through me to things; and all who love them go through me to things. Intelligence, give me the exact name—your name and theirs, and my name—of things!

### You first

One must speak in such a way that although someone else, or many others, or an infinite number of people have said it before, it seems as though you said it first.

### Word

You can repeat a word in writing or speech as often as necessary. Repeating the exact word is no defect, no poverty. The synonyms are there for all to see in the dictionary.

The value of repetition depends on who does the repeating.

Never copy yourself.

Say it differently, but let it seem natural.

### Those who

There are those who repeat unconsciously what another says (extreme imperfection). And those who repeat it consciously. Those who consciously do not repeat it. And those who unconsciously do not repeat it (extreme perfection).

Rhetoric produces in me the loathing for anything that is hatefully useless, like sleeplessness late at night, like a medicine taken when we are healthy, like a lamp burning in the daytime, like a bed still made in the morning.

The annihilation of form through the perfection of form.

Formal perfection (simplicity, spontaneity) is neither vulgar neglect of form or the juggling act of some Baroque architect with a bad case of indigestion. In both cases, one gets tangled up in form, and at every moment it demands our attention and trips us up. It is, rather, the absolute exactitude that makes form disappear, leaving only the content. So that the form *is* the content ...

A horror of archaism. Pure present, fresh, agreeable!

### Orator

I cannot conceive of a god who is an orator.

When god speaks softly, he is true; when he shouts, false.

How frightful, the house, the soul when empty—or full—of words.

A good, true, beautiful word soothes more than any special sedative.

Poetry is the almost said, literature the said, rhetoric the re-said. The almost said is the highest category of beauty.

When he speaks very badly or too well, man seems irrational, a pig or a canary; he only seems the man he is supposed to be when he expresses himself in his sufficient, daily language.

But "daily" here means so much! I think that if God were to speak, he would speak in ordinary language, even making mistakes at times.

## Padding

In rhymed verse, it is what you wouldn't say in free verse; in free verse, what you wouldn't say in ordinary prose; in ordinary prose, what you wouldn't say were you speaking exactly.

Much, yes, as long as it is as good as little.

The greatest of everything and of nothing has needed names no longer than: sun, faith, being, no, sea, light, yes, today, God, peace, voice, thirst, more, war.

To get it right, go back to the words of your mother.

### Farther and more spoken

Write the way you speak and you will go farther and be more spoken of than by writing the way you write.

Words, like waves and wings, are always virgin.

It matters nothing that the ideas we enunciate don't seem especially opportune. No matter how isolated and abstract they seem to us, they will come into their meaning, with a huge variety of unsuspected nuances, when the reader finds himself in a moral situation analogous to the one in which they were written.

## Style

I believe that when people talk about style they generally confuse substance with what is secondary. When they talk about style, they are talking about the word, and I believe that style is something which comes from the bottom of the soul. That is the drift of my aphorisms.

Style: the exact, the only expressive path for our being, the definitive discovery of the unbreakable thread in our living labyrinth. Our inexhaustible and pleasurable current.

Style: the path of someone with land, the current of someone with sea or river, the thread of someone with labyrinth.

Not to doodle uselessly, whimsically in the margins of reality.

Poetry, like fire, water, earth, the air like the universe, is neither masculine nor feminine. Or maybe masculine and feminine at the same time.

These sexual distinctions, used by bad minor critics, have nothing to do with poetry.

The word is made, was made, for the ear, not the eye. And

poetry comes in more at the ear than at the eye.

When we feel the impulse to write, let us not reason whether or not we ought to write this or that, but simply write it, for to write is to create. And later we can reason whether or not to "save" it.

"You write so much," I am told by lots of people who have written a single ridiculous little book, each of whose poems is like one of my commas.

They don't realize that for a true poet writing is like eating, a true necessity that, besides, like all necessities, is enjoyable.

## *More lost*

Friend, do not think about what has been lost of what you have written, but about what you have not written, which is much more lost for you.

# Revision

*¡Esta lucha constante entre querer acabar y querer acabar bien!*

—JRJ

NOT EVERYONE PURSUES perfection in writing, but work of all kinds involves a slow, final disposition of details—refining, purifying, polishing—and a moment of thought for how the work will be received.

To revise a text—to look at it again, slowly and lovingly—is, for some, the most pleasurable phase of work, and one of the deeper pleasures in life. But revision is not always mere looking. The work of "retouching" or "polishing" seems to arise, as Gaston Bachelard once noticed, from a certain primitive libidinal urge. He speaks of the continued "caress" of polishing; its "gentle, rhythmic, seductive moment." Juan Ramón, too, speaks of "caressing" his work and bestowing perfection on it, as though giving it "a big, round hug." And Virgil said that he gave birth to his poems and then, like a she-bear, licked them slowly into shape.

No modern poet can have devoted more thought to revision than Juan Ramón Jiménez. For him, creation and correction were the counterpoint of poetry, parts of one same, unending process. His work was always in progress. He came to think that his very earliest books, as books, were beyond salvation, and begged his friends and admirers to bring him copies, purchased at secondhand bookstalls or purloined from the National Library, which he destroyed or pulled apart, saving only the individual pages that might be rewritten and rearranged. Those pages, and other first, or second, or third drafts of poems sometimes went into boxes in the basement of his Madrid apartment buildings. They were the subsoil of his daily labor. When space became available, the boxes were carried up to his workroom, where dozens of different books in progress were spread out carefully on the floor and the furniture. He dreamed of a "simple, long, narrow pine table" where he could see before him seventy or eighty books he had already written and could fall "by surprise" on this or that poem, revise it and dictate a new version to Zenobia. To publish a poem was sometimes only a way of distancing himself from it: on the printed page, its defects always stood out more sharply than in his own peculiar script. Poems that had already appeared in books, magazines, and newspapers were "published drafts," grist for the mill.

At first he revised in his head. But over the years his methods changed. In 1931, for example, his friend Juan Guerrero Ruiz heard him explain

that he has decided not to do the final revision he used to do while lying on the sofa and working from memory, analyzing each text, one word after another, until leaving it completely finished. This used to involve a huge amount of mental work, and [he thinks that] perhaps it left the poems too pure, and now he has had a change of thought and understands that it is better to leave things a little unfinished, without that final phase of revision. "Better to leave the work a little fresher, though it be less perfect."

Juan Ramón's best-known poem –

> Touch it no more,
> The rose is like that.

—suggests that although there is no end to revision, there is a point when revision becomes "sufficient." "Perfect and imperfect, like the rose," he said in an aphorism. In another, addressed angrily to a critic, he adds, "When I say 'touch it no more,' I mean that I have already touched everything, even the rose!" and he was probably right: that little poem may have begun as part of a longer one, and, ignoring his own advice, he was to change it again before he died, turning the two lines into one.

What other insights did he acquire, over decades of reflection, about correction and revision? His aphorisms offer advice:

*Surprise your work.* Sneak up on it and revise it "by surprise," as though it were the work of someone else. Correct it as though you were a "surprised, intelligent reader" of yourself. Only from a psychological distance will you see your work clearly and take pleasure in it.

*Revise part of your work, but remember the whole.* When you correct a single work, you are revising something larger: all the work you have ever done and will ever do. "I revise neither page nor book, but Work." Juan Ramón tried to remember that, in rewriting even a paragraph, we are preparing another "draft" of the work of our entire lives. This

THE COMPLETE PERFECTIONIST

kept him from fretting endlessly over nuance.

*Correction is sometimes only confirmation.* You needn't always change the work, only "relive" it imaginatively, "confirm" it, "hear its confession," and send it on its way.

*Respect the person you were.* To revise intelligently, you must reckon with your former self—whoever it was who wrote that!—and try to balance "instinct" and critical intelligence. "Don't strike from your work the word you no longer understand. There was a reason you put it there."

*Respect the defect that cannot be conquered.* It is an irreducible element of your style, your "character."

*Take down the scaffolding.* Even after intensive revision, finished work should seem fresh and spontaneous, without a trace of the labor that went into it. The Spaniard Lope de Vega, who wrote over a thousand plays, once said that he wanted "the rough draft very dark and the ideas very clear." After revising a poem, Juan Ramón liked to destroy the rough draft, "making fun of the future philologist."

Paul Valéry famously remarked that poems are never finished, only abandoned. The quality of revision depends on the instinct and the intelligence that go into that abandonment, and the thought taken for the people who will find the abandoned work: how they will use it, what will become of it. Some poems are abandoned with remorse; others in boredom or desperation. Juan Ramón wanted to abandon each of his poems with all the intelligence and love that went into their creation.

— ❋ —

Impossible last week of each work!

This constant struggle between wanting to be finished and wanting to finish well!

After having written lyrical poems sufficient—in quantity, quality and character—to make a book, there is a different art altogether, that of forming the book. A book of lyrical poems has to be enchanting, like a field or a garden, with grace and harmonious disorder, or ordered freedom. Here and there there are light, little paths that empty quickly into others, groups of trees or vines, water to reflect, just for a moment, something successive, brief silent stories or fragments of beautiful stories. And one also has to take into account the color the poems acquire according to the spot they occupy, and the accent.

Accent and defect are what defines a poet's personality.

A work is fully corrected and purified when we have reread it and relived it, and it gives the full, exact impression of its life at the instant it was created.

I want any of my books to be opened anywhere and reveal something exact.

Lazy writers and stupid critics often say that one cannot correct what one wrote in the past because it would falsify emotions and feelings. This is merely a question of skill. One can recapture the spirit of a poem already written just as well as that of a landscape or an event from the past. Don't people write about the past?

### Contrary beauty

When I was young, I used to prefer the autumn, night, and the moon. Now, old, I prefer the day, the sun, and spring.

It was, and is, logical for a poet always to like contrary beauty.

Nothing more vain and absurd than to correct with "a will to finish."

### Over one's work

To go back over one's work—or not to—is only a problem of love.

How expect others to love our work if we do not feel immense love for it ourselves?

No delight you lavish on your work will be wasted on it.

### One day after another

Whoever doesn't relive his work one day after another risks having others see in it beauties and secrets that he himself ignores. As though someone else were able to see in our mothers, wives, or daughters what we ourselves were unable to see.

In our work, there can be something we haven't seen, but nothing we haven't looked at.

## Inspection

To create with all the senses of the soul and the body. And to correct with one sense only, that of sight, the eye.

Because what is given to us, intimately, by the god of the moment cannot be corrected. And what remains, when the god of that instant has vanished, is only "inspection."

## All of a sudden

To correct something, return to it all of a sudden. Catch it alone and stark naked.

When we correct, it should be as if we were intelligent, surprised readers of ourselves.

## Order

To correct: give order to surprise.

## Surprise

For me, the supreme virtue in life, in the realm both of the useful and the beautiful is surprise... When revising my poetry, which I am continually stroking and caressing, I have always corrected by surprise. Somewhere in my workplace (table, chair, floor) I leave the poem or note I have begun. I look lovingly at them for a moment, without being too hard on them or on myself. And then I go away, taking them away to a spot in true memory ...For possible expression is every-where: on the page, in the atmosphere, anyplace in the house.

And when I go back to that expression, which is expecting me and which, without a doubt, knows what I am bringing to it, the expression rises up to me and yields up its secret, its life. And thus what I give to the text—or better, what the text gives me—what we give to each other—is surprise.

One must catch life and death by surprise. Everything beautiful in life and death is best seen that way. Maybe death and life need a method, but the method must be surprising, must be in love with surprise. Technique must be warm, jumpy, vital. Nothing uglier than the unknown but expected face; nothing lovelier than the familiar or strange face caught by surprise.

Surprise leaps over everything and over us with the naked emotion of erect feeling, of spirit.

As long as one of my books is missing one last word, one last comma, it still absorbs me. Once I've inserted that comma, it falls away to my left like lead. Then, when time has gone by and the book is forgotten, it begins to fly again like a butterfly, stand like a rose, and I am charmed again by it. But for the moment I hate it, and am only charmed by the new.

If one reads (corrects) very slowly, the language becomes disjointed and ends up saying nothing.

Correction can only be rapid and successive. Anything else would paralyze writing.

When one tries too hard with a poem (a painting, a piece

of music), the poem vanishes. because final, true, invariable, incorrigible perfection lies in nothingness, *nada*.

### Any meaning at all

When we correct our writing, it is enough to find there a meaning: any of the innumerable meanings it can have, although the meaning be different or have a different nuance from the one we thought it had when it was created.

### Nuances

Take it from me: there is no greater madness than that of the madman of "nuances."

### Successive axiom

No day... without erasing a line and tearing up some paper or other.

No page is too insignificant not to be torn up.

In the papers in my wastebasket, what beauties of rhythm and color! What a restless, dull kaleidoscope!

When you wonder whether one version is better than the other, don't lose time arguing with yourself. Leave them both.

### Savior

We live from, and with, what we save.

For me all the world is divided into two parts: one where there might be papers of mine, and one where there are none. How restful, the second!

I would like to live for another year after my death without the power to create anything new, simply revise the work I have already completed.

To correct is not to exhaust and not to kill; it is to make the work complete, to leave it alive forever.

When correcting, I have tried to respect the *accent*.

How to bring together the ecstatic and the dynamic?

A dynamic ecstasy.

When we correct, let us think that we will never conclude; that we aren't doing, will never do, anything definitive.

Refining a work need not necessarily mean modifying (transforming). A poem can be perfectly refined—and this is frequent in my poetry—without having undergone the least change. To refine it was only to have it scrupulously examine its conscience and then have the pleasure of finding it (without defects) perfect.

### Second fitting

In most cases, my corrections are like a successful second fitting.

Since there is no end to correction, let it simply be sufficient.

Let us not forget that some defects are invincible. It is these that give the defect its perpetuity and prestige. Exactness lies in conquering the six conquerable defects and respecting the seventh, the only invincible one.

How wonderful it feels, after so much effort, to leave things just the way they were.

What has been well revised in the morning... how beautifully "classical" (eternal) it seems in the evening.

Let our work be free of us: the scaffolding burnt, the future philologist made fun of: naked, smooth and round, nothing sticking to it, like an egg—from what bird? like a seed—from what plant?—, like Venus on her shell.

### Doubletree

Let the finished book go on quivering with emotion and intelligence, a clean arrow newly and forever fixed into the double tree of life and art.

Complete: perfect and imperfect in equilibrium.

# Perfection

*Era casi perfecta. su mejor encanto estaba en el "casi".*

—JRJ

JUAN RAMÓN'S IDEA of perfection departs from the common meaning of the word and emphasizes process more than product. For him, something perfect is something that is becoming complete and completely *becoming*: a thing moving slowly and successively into its own, helped along, in the case of art, by instinct and intelligent reflection. Perfection means gradual movement toward an ideal intuited in creative reverie or, as Juan Ramón puts it, in "the well-nourished subconscious." Two paradigms of perfection in nature are the star, because as it burns, it seems to be "always making itself"; and the rose, which is perfect because of—not despite—its imperfections. When perfection and imperfection are in balance, art and work reach plenitude and sensual fullness. Juan Ramón speaks of the "sufficient infinite" of the rose. *Just enough* infinity, just the right dose of eternity!

How unbearable eternity would be if it lasted more than one or two or three minutes. As unbearable as a long poem, a mass, a whole night of lovemaking, a rosary. Prayer, love, poetry, all of the highest moments in life, are eternal if they are beautiful and fleeting. Eternity is a conception of the bored and wistful person.

Perfection is neither being "completely finished" nor being "totally free of defects." For Juan Ramón, that sort of perfection is "poison." The defect, when it is a beautiful, fatal gift of inspiration, is what gives an object its own memorable character, rescuing it from sameness. Inconsistency is the enemy of quality, but not of perfection, as Juan Ramón conceives of it:

> Yes, inconsistent. Like all natural and supernatural forces: water, air, fire, earth, the flesh, light, love, the rose, grace, joy, pain.

In short, perfection is dynamic and successive: a poem moving toward its plenitude. No wonder that Juan Ramón seized delightedly on an expression he had seen in American and English poets: "work in progress." To him, work no longer "in progress" can move no one, not even its creator. Something truly perfect gives the feeling of imminence, of being just about to happen. Perfection is always being realized, and even when it is abandoned, the perfect poem will continue, always, to "quiver with emotion and intelligence." Perfection is approximation. It is "penultimate imperfection," the "always of never." In poetry and in any creative work, there is always another step, leading to boredom and sterility, and it is better not to take it.

—— ❋ ——

Simplicity, freshness, purity, sharpness, synthesis… perfection.

Perfect, but natural.

The infinitely small, when it reaches a certain point of perfection, is as great as the infinitely large.

### (and)

Much (and) perfect. The secret, the little problem is in the "*and.*"

The best is no enemy of the good, says the Spanish proverb. But it is.

Bad is closer to good than is mediocre.

Careful, friends, every day we confuse rhetoric with perfection!

### From the very root

Perfection comes from the very root of the well-nourished subconscious and a little at random, likes the flower.

The best art always gives a surprising, somewhat alien first impression, as absolute beauty would give. And then comes mutual conquest, and we are saved: the extraordinary makes us extraordinary.

In any work that is complete, the perfect and the imperfect must "exist" in equilibrium, each with its perpetual, unavoidable, demanding beautiful reality.

Perfect and imperfect, like the rose.

## Defect

I like the defect. And thus prefer to find it rather than to remove, diminish, or emend it. What I try to avoid is excess.

Defect—something like a verb ending or a declension, not immorality or ugliness.

Finding the defect is a matter of luck, as when you get something right. You don't search for it, you simply come upon it.

## Character

When perfection is impossible, search for character, which is almost always more, and never less, than perfection.

Poor lover of perfection, don't you see that you are a living poet and that life is undying imperfection?

What perfects you kills you. Without a doubt, perfection is poison.

The truly definitive is nothing but the exactly provisional.

## Not another step

Perfection is penultimate imperfection.
Not another step if we want to stay alive. *"The rose is like that."*

What a struggle between charm and perfection. Charming perfection, perfect charm.

## In the "almost"

Almost perfect: its greatest charm was in the "almost."

A work of art is imperfect when, in form, the beautiful rushes ahead of the exact. Perfect when the exact and the beautiful coincide. But even better when the exact dominates the beautiful.

I do not believe in perfection. I would believe in "impossible successive perfection," as in "possible, successive imperfection."

## Always a never

The perfect—that is the complete—is always a never; I mean, the never of always.

———— ❋ ————

# *Afterword*

*…es siempre un nunca, es decir, un nunca de siempre.*

—JRJ

———— ❋ ————

*... the never of always.*

DID HE EVER find perfection?

He hoped to create a Book so perfectly beautiful that it would return the universe to silence and oneness. One book, his *Obra*, the Work to end all poetic work! He thought of that book as an ideal world and of himself as its god. Unlike the Maker he was emulating, he could not simply will that world into existence: "the only way to perfection is through imperfection." He tried to believe that it would arise "successively" from the imperfection of life, out of the unitary rhythm of each day's work, led by instinct, refreshed by dream, helped by intelligence, and instructed by nature. When we consider his poems, prose, and books of poems, many seem perfect, and not merely as fragments. It is only when we remember the impossible goal he set for himself—the creation of a unitary Work—that we can speak of failure.

He was a victim of his own abundance, unable to gather all that he planted. He wrote tirelessly for more than six decades, and even with the help of Zenobia who served him until a few days before she died, he was unable to "relive," revise, arrange, and publish all that he had saved of all that he had written. "Much and perfect. In the *and* lies the secret, the little problem." Or rather, the crux of his existence.

He was the god, not the savior, of his work. Troubled by its abundance and diffuseness, he tried to console himself:

> I don't want people to read everything I have written. It is enough for some to read some things, and others other things, reading here and there. My passion is for my readers to be here and there in my work, but wherever their eyes rest, to find perfect beauty.

He searched for what is impossible either to write or to read—the perfect Work—and left, in his writing, an ardent defense of solitude and "invisible reality": dream and instinct, ecstasy and sorrow, gratitude and, above all, desire. We may say of him, using his own expression, that he "burned completely":

> In this world of ours we must burn completely. Each of us must resolve himself completely in the flames, in the resolution that belongs to him alone. No Creator, no god that we can create could possibly accept those who do not fulfill their lives completely...

He "burned completely" in the flame of his daily work, pursuing, and not achieving, what he wanted. On the way to his impossible goal, he inspired others—his "immense minority"—to work, and to have faith in work. He found truths that mattered more than the goal. He discovered that "God is not the origin or the end, he is the middle"; that

> the value of a work lies not in its end, in its "rounding off," but in the open, prickly, spiritual and material vibration caused by its never-ending restlessness.

He liked beginnings and middles, not endings; odds, not evens. He liked sharp, pointy things rather than round ones (the aphorism is both.) He discovered that poetry and perfection are always *becoming*, and came to accept that his own work was "work in progress, imagination in movement, poetic succession." And perhaps this is his best lesson—the one he lived most intensely—about poetry, work, and perfection. He teaches that an impossible goal creates a possible path, a present where we can "burn completely, holding nothing back, spending all of our strength on our *trabajo gustoso*, whatever it happens to be. In one of his earliest aphorisms, he wrote:

> The world does not need to come from a god. For better or worse, the world is here. But it does need to go to one (where is he?), and that is why the poet exists.

The poet leads us, forever, toward the mystery of perfection. Poetry, he wrote, is the "phenomenon that sets our being in motion." And so it is with perfection. It is never "had," never "realized" by anybody. It always escapes. By defending the impossible, the poet helps it do so.

# SOURCES & ACKNOWLEDGMENTS

THANKS TO Carmen Hernández-Pinzón for permission to prepare this second, revised edition of *The Complete Perfectionist*, with aphorisms that had not been published in 1997. Thanks, across the years, to those who helped with the first edition (New York: Doubleday Currency, 1997): Francisco Hernández-Pinzón, Harriet Rubin, Jennifer Breheny, Lisa Brancaccio, Bob Daniels, María Estrella Iglesias, Efraín Kristal, Robert Bly. Special thanks to my publisher David Rade.

*The Complete Perfectionist* (the title, theme, selection, translation, and arrangement of which are my own) draws on several works by Juan Ramón Jiménez (=JRJ). The aphorisms are from Antonio Sánchez Romeralo's splendid edition of *Ideolojía (1897-1957)* (Barcelona: Anthropos, 1990), which includes 4,116 of them, and (in this second edition) the supplementary volume, *Ideolojía II (=I2)*, edited and annotated by Emilio Ríos (Moguer: Ediciones de la Fundación JRJ/ Casa Zenobia y Juan Ramón, 1998). I have also consulted *Río Arriba: Selección de aforismos*, edited by Juan Varo Zafra in the multivolume series of *Obras de Juan Ramón Jiménez* (Madrid: Visor Libros, 2007) and have gathered biographical information in the collections of Juan Ramón's papers at the Archivo Histórico Nacional (Madrid) and, with help from its efficient director Carmen L. Busquet, the Sala Zenobia/JRJ at the Universidad de Puerto Rico, Río Piedras.

There is no complete critical edition in Spanish of Juan Ramón's poetry. The most recent approximation is *Obra poética* (=*OP*), 2 vols. edited by Javier Blasco and Teresa Gómez Trueba (Madrid: Espasa-Calpe/Biblioteca de Literatura Universal, 2005). See also Sánchez Romeralo's edition of *Poesías últimas escojidas (1918-1958)* (Madrid: Espasa-Calpe, 1982) (= *PUE*); his edition of *Leyenda (1896-1956)* , 2nd ed., with notes by María Estela Harretche (Madrid: Visor, 2006); and his clear and helpful introduction and notes to *La realidad invisible (1917-1920 1924) Libro inédito* (London: Tamesis Books, 1983). Over the past few years, all of Juan Ramón's published books have been appearing in paperback in the *Obras* series published by Visor, with each title introduced by a Spanish poet.

There are admirable historic translations of Jiménez's poetry by James Wright in *Above the River: The Complete Poems* (New York: Wesleyan University Press/Farrar, Straus and Giroux/University Press of New England, 1990), pp. 87-90; and by Robert Bly, a steady defender of Jiménez's work since the late 1950s, in *Lorca and Jiménez: Selected Poems* (Boston: Beacon Press, 1973). See Bly's *American Poetry: Wildness and Domesticity* (New York: Harper and Row, 1991), where he compares the poetry of Jiménez polemically to that of American poets and associates it with a "new imagination" that can revitalize English-language poetry. Antonio

T. de Nicolas has published three volumes of Jiménez's later work, with prefaces by Louis Simpson: *Time and Space: A Poetic Autobiography*, *God Desired and Desiring*, and *Invisible Reality* (Paragon House, 1986-87). There is a translation by Myra C. Livingston and Josef F. Domínguez of *Platero y yo* (Boston: Houghton Mifflin, 1994), and a recent *Selected Poems* by Salvador Ortiz-Carboneres (Aris and Phillips, 2005), though no book has yet supplanted the *Selected Writings* translated many decades ago by H.R. Hays (Farrar, Straus and Cudahy, 1957). In 2004, Hugh Harter brought out the first complete edition in English *of Diary of a Newlywed Poet*, with an excellent introduction by Jiménez scholar Michael Predmore (Cranbury, NJ: Associated University Presses).

There is no detailed biography in English. The most complete in Spanish is Graciela Palau de Nemes, *Vida y obra de JRJ: La poesía desnuda*, 2nd ed. (Madrid: Gredos, 1974). Juan Guerrero Ruiz's *Juan Ramón de viva voz*, in its second, augmented edition in two volumes edited by Manuel Ruiz-Funes Fernández (Valencia: Pre-Textos/Museo Ramón Gaya, 1998) records JRJ's daily pronouncements on poetry and poets, and on his own work, 1913-36. The *Diario* of Juan Ramón's intelligent and energetic wife, Zenobia Camprubí, three volumes of which have been carefully edited by Palau de Nemes, gives a vivid picture of their life in exile. Alfonso Alegre Heitzmann has begun publishing Juan Ramón's complete letters, beginning with *Epistolario*, vol. I, 1898-1916 (Madrid: Publicaciones de la Residencia de Estudiantes, 2006).

The notes that follow cover (1) works cited in the introduction and in the essays preceding each series of aphorisms; (2) sources of the aphorisms and short poems translated here.

Most of the poems exist in different versions in the original; Sánchez Romeralo and other editors provide ample information. Unless otherwise indicated, page numbers refer to *Ideolojía*. I have sometimes omitted the titles of the shorter aphorisms.

## INTRODUCTION (PP. 1-16)

"When I publish a book..." *Leyenda* 25; "Let us think," 265; "Mankind has become," 186; "How close to the soul..." in *Obra poética* II, book 2: 60. "It seems more logical" 394; "I want to look" 283; "I dreamed for our language..." 83. Aphorisms on Spain 351-53 and 401. On Shelley: Howard T. Young, *The Line in the Margin* (Madison: University of Wisconsin Press, 1980): 63. "Constant, endless fervor.,.." *OP* I, book 2: 640. On JRJ and his disciples, *Lorca and Jiménez: Selected Poems,* p. 3 and *Ideolojía* 546. On JRJ's plans for publishing his work, Guerrero Ruiz, *passim.* "I would like my book..." in *OP* I, book 2: 537; on "unwritten poetry" 461, 503; "Let no one take advice" 453; "Art is not" 145; "Between each two ideas" 638; "When I don't" 381; Rainer Maria Rilke, *Rodin,* tr. Robert Firmage (Salt Lake City: Peregrine Smith, 1979): 95.

## SELF (PP. 17-26)

"My kingdom" 299; "Let us cultivate" 186; names given by mother 259; "I no longer trust" 533; "To live is to create" 656; "To poetize" 123. "I am not I..." in Bly, *Lorca and Jiménez* 77; *OP* I, book 2: 418; later version in *Leyenda* 625. Aphorisms: 278, 201, *I2* 116, 422, 185, 559, 84, 205, 253, 25, 300, 300, 96, 37, 254, 287, *Realidad invisible* 117, 165, *I2* 123, 727, 67, 985, 460.

## RHYTHM (PP. 27-37)

Simone Weil, *The Simone Weil Reader*, ed. George A. Pani-
chas (New York: David McKay, 1977): 61; "I cannot divide"
338; "That day.." *OP* I, book 2: 604-05. Aphorisms: 251,
338, 20, 902, 509, 104, 337, *I*2 100, 147, 338, 123, 337, 337, 224,
"If you go quickly" *OP* I, book 2: 413. *I*2 100, *I*2 100, 80, 394,
231, 235, 302, 125, 87, 399, 451, 94, 239, 139, 302, 97, 299, 250.

## SILENCE (PP. 39-49)

"With silence, I bind" *I*2 108. On JRJ and Shakespeare, see
Carmen Pérez Romero, *Juan Ramón Jiménez y la poesía an-
glosajona* (Cáceres: Universidad de Extremadura, 1992): 46.
"My effort" 288; Parrots *I*2 123; Guerrero, *JR de viva voz*, 1st
ed. (Madrid: Insula, 1961): 243 (cricket) and 365 (changes of
apartment). "El grillo real" ("The Real Cricket"), in *OP* II,
book 2: 817-18: 191-92. On creating noise, 346. Aphorisms:
381, 188, 25, 418, 345, 345, 344, *I*2 106, *I*2 106, 22, 233, 123, 655,
123, *I*2 107, *I*2 107, *I*2 108, 588, 189, 202, 345, 345, 344 , 344,
345, 465, 346, 188, 184, 346, 233.

## THE PRESENT (PP. 51-56)

Samuel Johnson, *Rambler* article, Tuesday, August 7, 1750,
in *Works*, vol. 4, ed. Arthur Murphy (London: Joyce Gold,
1806), p. 239; "We have been...", *Realidad invisible* 223; "Care
for this day..." in *Libros de poesía*, ed. Augustín Caballero
(Madrid: Aguilar, 1959): 204. Aphorisms: 235, *I*2 96, *I*2 96,
*I*2 97, 244-45, 649, 492, 408, 334, 184, 334, 335, 34, 139, 188,
336, 241, 486, 487, 333, 335, 337, 334, 336, 335. "Light," *PUE*

102; "I awoke..." *OP* I, book 2: 747.

## MEMORY (PP. 59-64)

"My ideal" 340; "seven plagues" 70. Aphorisms: 641, 131, 131, 339, 340, 340, 340, 290, *I*2 90, 184, 339, 148, 382; "Memory", *PUE* 104; 335-36, 585, 641, 642, *I*2 90, 195.

## IDEALS (PP. 65-71)

Sir Philip Sidney, *An Apology for Poetry*, ed. Forrest G. Robinson (New York: Macmillan, 1986): 17, 22. "Sevillian Gardener," *Política poética* 25. Aphorisms: 121, 157, 689, 572, 21, 121, 153, 467, 249, 582, 395, 128, 610, 588, 284, 291, 644.

## NATURE (PP. 73-84)

Sidney, *Apology*, p. 17. Ralph Waldo Emerson, "The Poet," in *Essays*, ed. Irwin Edman (New York: Crowell, 1926): 278, 398. "No matter" 392; "If we look" 604; Rilke, *Rodin* 96. "What do I care" *Política poética*, ed. G. Bleiberg (Madrid: Alianza Editorial, 1982): 173; Emerson, "Nature," in *Essays*, p. 398; "This is my life" *OP* I, book 2: 612. Aphorisms: 60, 691, 141, 392, 190, 455, *I*2 88, 709, 72, 260, 342, 634, 409, 262, 363, 503, 483, 199, 518, 194, 194, 402, 248, 262, 416, 667, 342, 391, 516, 342, 387, *I*2 83, 118; "White cloud..." *OP* I, book 2: 631; 118.

## INSTINCT (PP. 85-92)

William Morris, quoted in Carl Fehrman, *Poetic Creation: Inspiration or Craft*, tr. Karin Petherick (Minneapolis: University of Minnesota, 1980):. 75. Edgar Allan Poe, *Complete Works*, vol. 14, ed. James A. Harrison (New York: Crowell, 1902): 195. Paul Valéry, "I seek a word..." in Fehrman, *Poetic Creation* 87; Rilke, *Rodin*, p. 89. Aphorisms: 152, 97, 320, 243, 380, 51, 409, 20, 567, 22, 160, 394, 171, 167, 27, 247, 262, 144, 187, 97, 171.

## DREAM (PP. 93-102)

Bly, *American Poetry* 5; cf. "Mares" in *Segunda antología poética* (Madrid: Espasa Calpe 1969), p. 494. "Power who use me" *Leyenda* 680;. "The poem calls to me..."*Tiempo y Espacio*, ed. Arturo del Villar (Madrid: Edaf, 1986): 168. Aphorisms: 430, 283, 124, 140, "Harbor" *OP* I, book 2: 788; "My hand deep inside" *Leyenda* 651; 124, 407-08, 124, 123, 123, 396, 658, 691; "How very sad...!" *Tiempo y Espacio* 166; 118, 413, 107, 685, 568, 684; "Sleepless" *Leyenda* 674; "Above and Below Our Death" *Tiempo y Espacio* 169; 90, 132.

## DEATH (PP. 103-111)

Miguel de Unamuno, *Del sentimiento trágico de la vida* (Madrid: Alianza, 1986): 252. "The Work" *Realidad invisible* 95; Guerrero Ruiz, *Juan Ramón de viva voz*, 1st ed. 329; "Light and Shadow" *Leyenda* 517. Francisco de Quevedo, *OP*, ed. José Manuel Blecua (Madrid: Editorial Castalia, 1989): 184-85; "What happens..." *OP* I, book 2: 626; "Ah, sleep" *OP* I, book 2: 591-92. Aphorisms: 319, 118-19, 318-23, 655, 657, 721. "At times I love", *Realidad invisible* 141.

## WRITING (PP. 113-123)

There is a phonograph recording of JRJ reading another version of the poem by Abu-Said Ibn Abil-Kheir (967-1049): *Archivo de la Palabra* (Madrid: Publicaciones de la Residencia de Estudiantes). On "literature" and "poetry": *Política poética* 83. Unamuno, *Del sentimiento trágico* 253. "This or that person..." 192. "Intelligence, give me..." complete version in *Leyenda* 605. Aphorisms: 408, 579, 520, 602, 81, 60, 381, 211, 264, 264, 387, 76, 359, 68, 218, 514, 659, 418, 230, 580, 696, 550, 262, 445, 123, 160, 198, 129, 220, 177, 396, 445, 445, 239, I2 76, 741.

## REVISION (PP. 125-137)

Gaston Bachelard, *The Psychoanalysis of Fire*, tr. Alan C. M. Ross (Boston: Beacon Press, 1964): 30-31. methods of revision, Guerrero Ruiz, 1st ed. 131; "Touch it no more..." as two lines in *Segunda antología* 242 and as one in *Leyenda* 647; Aphorisms: 241, 298, I2 14, I2 17, 123, I2 19, I2 53, I2 99, 389, 158, 249, 240, 298, 577, 688, 175, 606, 500, 249, 424, 606, 464, 284, 21, 189, 242, 246, 147, 520, 89, 247, 470, 249, I2 88, 144, 572, 296, 241, 196, 205, 182, 187.

## PERFECTION (PP. 139-145)

"How unbearable" 647; "Inconsistent" 300; Aphorisms: 261,

268, 331, 166, 237, 397, 214, 685, 23, 198, 190, 952, 198, 411, 417, 203, 540, 237, 546, 293, 171, 401, 609, 700.

## AFTERWORD (PP. 147-151)

"I don't want" 244; "In this world" *Política poética* 404; "God is not" 326, 443; "The world does not need" 33.

SWAN ISLE PRESS is an independent, not-for-profit, literary publisher dedicated to publishing works of poetry, fiction and nonfiction that inspire and educate while advancing the knowledge and appreciation of literature, art, and culture. The Press's bilingual editions and single-language English translations make contemporary and classic texts more accessible to a variety of readers.

For more information on books of related interest or for a catalog of new publications contact:

*www.swanislepress.com*

THE COMPLETE PERFECTIONIST

Designed by Andrea Guinn
Typeset in Caslon
Printed on 55# Glatfelter Natural

S  W  A  N
I  S  L  E
P  R  E  S  S